EUROVISION
A GRAND DESIGN

THE COMPLETE HISTORY OF EUROPE'S ICONIC SONG CONTEST

FLORENCE FLETCHER

Copyright © 2025 Florence Fletcher

All rights reserved. No part of this publication may be reproduced, distributed, or transmitted in any form or by any means, including photocopying, recording, or other electronic or mechanical methods, without the prior written permission of the publisher, except in the case of brief quotations embodied in critical reviews and certain other noncommercial uses permitted by copyright law.

ISBN: 9798307787724

Independently Published

Cover design by FAB Designs

CONTENTS

Copyright
Introduction: The Eurovision Phenomenon — 1
Chapter 1: The Birth of a Continental Contest (1956-1959) — 4
Chapter 2: Eurovision in the Swinging Sixties (1960-1969) — 12
Chapter 3: Eurovision in the Disco Era (1970-1979) — 20
Chapter 4: Eurovision in the Age of New Wave and Power Ballads (1980-1989) — 26
Chapter 5: Eurovision in the Post-Cold War Era (1990-1999) — 34
Chapter 6: Eurovision in the New Millennium (2000-2009) — 44
Chapter 7: Eurovision in the Age of Social Media (2010-2019) — 53
Chapter 8: Eurovision in the Pandemic Era and Beyond (2020-Present) — 62
Chapter 9: Behind the Curtain — 75
Chapter 10: The Politics of Eurovision — 81
Chapter 11: Eurovision's Technological Evolution — 86
Chapter 12: Eurovision's Effect on Popular Music — 90
Chapter 13: Eurovision and European Identity — 97
Chapter 14: The Future of Eurovision — 103
Chapter 15: The Enduring Appeal of Eurovision — 108
Close - The Heart of Eurovision — 113

INTRODUCTION: THE EUROVISION PHENOMENON

I n a dazzling spectacle of music, culture, and occasional kitsch, the Eurovision Song Contest has captivated audiences for nearly seven decades. What began as an ambitious experiment in live television broadcasting has evolved into a global event, uniting millions of viewers in a shared experience that transcends borders and languages.

Since its inception in 1956 with just seven participating countries, Eurovision has grown into a global phenomenon. Today, it features over 40 nations and commands a worldwide audience that would have been unimaginable to its founders. By 1965, the contest was already reaching an estimated 150 million viewers, a testament to its rapid rise in popularity and cultural significance.

This book aims to provide a comprehensive and entertaining exploration of Eurovision's rich history, from its post-war origins to its current status as a glitter-bombed extravaganza. We'll delve into the contest's cultural significance, examining how it has shaped (and been shaped by) European identity. We'll trace the technological advancements that have transformed Eurovision from a modest radio show with cameras to a state-of-the-art production viewed by millions worldwide.

Through iconic moments, behind-the-scenes stories, and analysis of its impact on popular music and politics, we'll uncover how Eurovision has become much more than just a song contest. It's a cultural institution that has played a unique role in fostering a sense of European unity while simultaneously highlighting the continent's diverse tapestry of cultures – all set to a soundtrack of power ballads and pop anthems.

As we embark on this journey through Eurovision's history, we'll explore:

- The contest's origins in post-war Europe and its evolution over the decades
- The politics of Eurovision, from voting blocs to on-stage protests
- The technological innovations that have shaped the contest (hello, wind machines!)
- Eurovision's influence on popular music and the careers it has launched
- The contest's role in shaping and reflecting European identity
- Behind-the-scenes stories from organizers, performers, and fans
- The future of Eurovision in an era of streaming and global entertainment

Whether you're a die-hard fan who can recite every winner since 1956, or a curious newcomer wondering why grown adults are so excited about a singing competition, this book offers a deep dive into one of the world's most unique and enduring cultural phenomena. So sit back, cue the dramatic key change, and let's explore the grand design that is the Eurovision Song Contest.

CHAPTER 1: THE BIRTH OF A CONTINENTAL CONTEST (1956-1959)

In the aftermath of World War II, a continent lay in ruins, both physically and spiritually. As Europe began the long process of rebuilding, there was a pressing need for initiatives that could foster unity and cooperation among nations that had so recently been bitter enemies. It was against this backdrop that the idea for what would become the Eurovision Song Contest first took shape – because it was felt that such a competition could provide some light relief and friendly competition.

The European Broadcasting Union (EBU) was formed in 1950, bringing together the public service broadcasters of Western Europe. This organization would prove instrumental in the creation of Eurovision. The EBU's initial focus was on news exchange and the development of a continental transmission network that could facilitate the sharing of programming across borders.

In 1954, the EBU achieved a significant milestone with the successful transmission of Queen Elizabeth II's coronation across the "Eurovision transmission network." This technological feat sparked the imagination of EBU executives, who began to envision more ambitious projects that could harness the power of this new network.

It was during a committee meeting in Monaco in January 1955 that the seed of Eurovision was planted. Italian television executive Sergio Pugliese, inspired by the success of Italy's Sanremo Music Festival, proposed the idea of a pan-European singing contest. The suggestion was met with enthusiasm from his colleagues, who saw in it the potential to showcase the capabilities of the Eurovision network while promoting international collaboration and friendly competition among European nations.

Marcel Bezençon, then President of the EBU Programme Committee, played a crucial role in turning this idea into reality. He championed the concept and worked tirelessly to bring it to fruition, earning him the unofficial title of "Father of the Eurovision Song Contest" (though "Glitter Papa" might have been more fitting).

The Swiss delegation, eager to demonstrate their broadcasting prowess, offered to host the inaugural event. Thus, the stage was set for the birth of what would become one of Europe's most beloved traditions.

On May 24, 1956, the Teatro Kursaal in Lugano, Switzerland, played host to the first Eurovision Song Contest. Seven countries participated in this groundbreaking event: Belgium, France, Germany, Italy, Luxembourg, the Netherlands, and Switzerland. In a format unique to this first edition, each country presented two songs, resulting in a total of 14 performances. The rules stipulated that only solo performers were allowed, a restriction that would soon be lifted in subsequent years.

The inaugural contest was a modest affair by today's standards, lasting approximately 1 hour and 40 minutes – a brevity that future Eurovision producers would look back on with wistful sighs. Swiss television presenter Lohengrin Filipello hosted the event, speaking entirely in Italian. This linguistic choice would be the first of many instances where language would play a significant role in Eurovision's history. As the performances concluded and the jury deliberated, the audience was treated to interval acts by Les Joyeux Rossignols and Les Trois Ménestrels. Finally, jury president Rolf Liebermann announced the winner: "Refrain," performed by Lys Assia, representing the host country Switzerland.

Assia's victory was not without drama. During her reprise performance, overcome with emotion, she momentarily forgot the lyrics and had to request a restart from the orchestra. This human moment set the stage for countless memorable Eurovision performances to come, reminding viewers of the high-stakes, live nature of the contest. While the full voting results of this first contest have been lost to time (presumably buried under a pile of discarded sequins – it's a shame, I'd love to know if they were as controversial then as they are now), reports suggest that Switzerland's winning entry received 102 points, with the second-place song finishing just two points behind. This close competition foreshadowed the nail-biting voting sequences that would become a hallmark of Eurovision in later years.

The success of the 1956 contest paved the way for Eurovision's rapid expansion. In 1957, the United Kingdom, Austria, and Denmark joined the competition, followed by Sweden in 1958. This growth brought new challenges and necessitated changes to the contest's format. The two-songs-per-country rule was abandoned in favor of one song each, and time limits were introduced to keep the show's length manageable. Another significant development came in 1958 when the principle of host country rotation was established. This decision ensured that the contest would travel across Europe, showcasing different cultures and broadcasting prowess. It also added an extra incentive for countries to strive for victory, as winning meant the prestige of hosting the following year's event (and the chance to show off their unique ability to build a stage that looked like it came straight out of a sci-fi B-movie).

The early years of Eurovision saw several memorable performances and influential artists. The Dutch singer Corry Brokken became the first artist to participate in the contest three years in a row (1956-1958), winning in 1957 with "Net als toen." In 1958, Italian singer Domenico Modugno captivated audiences with "Nel blu dipinto di blu," better known as "Volare." Although the song only placed third in the contest, it went on to become an international hit, topping the US Billboard Hot 100 and winning two Grammy Awards. This early example of Eurovision launching international careers would be repeated many times in the decades to come.

Behind the scenes, the contest faced numerous technical challenges. Broadcasting a live event across multiple countries was a formidable task in the 1950s, requiring careful coordination and cutting-edge technology. It was a bit like trying to herd cats, if the cats were wearing sequined bow ties and insisted on singing in different languages. Despite occasional glitches, these early broadcasts helped push the boundaries of what was possible in international television production. The cultural impact of Eurovision was evident from the start. The contest provided a unique platform for cultural exchange, allowing Europeans to experience music and performances from neighboring countries in an era when international travel was still a luxury for many. It also reflected the changing musical landscape of the late 1950s, with entries ranging from traditional ballads to more contemporary pop styles. Language quickly became a central issue in Eurovision. In these early years, countries were free to perform in any language, leading to a diverse linguistic landscape. This policy would change several times over the contest's history, becoming a point of contention and debate about national identity and cultural representation.

As the 1950s drew to a close, Eurovision had firmly established itself as a beloved annual tradition. The contest had already weathered changes in format, voting systems, and participating countries, setting the stage for even greater transformations in the decades to come. From these humble beginnings, a European cultural institution was born, one that would continue to captivate audiences and launch careers for generations to come.

The Eurovision Song Contest had transformed from an experimental broadcast into a cultural phenomenon, uniting millions of viewers across the continent. As Europe entered the 1960s, Eurovision was poised for further growth, ready to reflect and influence the rapidly changing cultural and political landscape of the continent – all while maintaining its unique blend of music, spectacle, and the occasional dash of glorious absurdity.

Eurovision Winners Of The 1950S

Year	Host City	Winner (Country)	Song Title
1956	Lugano	Lys Assia (Switzerland)	Refrain
1957	Frankfurt	Corry Brokken (Netherlands)	Net als toen
1958	Hilversum	André Claveau (France)	Dors, mon amour
1959	Cannes	Teddy Scholten (Netherlands)	Een beetje

Did You Know?

- The very first Eurovision Song Contest, held in Lugano, Switzerland, in 1956, featured a unique rule: each country could perform two songs. This rule was quickly abandoned due to the length of the show.

- Luxembourg's entry in 1956, "Ne crois pas," performed by Michèle Arnaud, holds the distinction of being the first-ever song performed in the Eurovision Song Contest.

- The 1958 contest was the first to include a "theme song" associated with the broadcast, called "Giorgio." Although it wasn't used every year following this, a version of this theme tune was developed and continues to be used by the contest today.

CHAPTER 2: EUROVISION IN THE SWINGING SIXTIES (1960-1969)

Beehives, bouffants, and a burgeoning sense of European unity. The 1960s: a decade of revolution—culturally, politically, and for Eurovision, musically. Never one to shy away from drama, the contest sashayed into the sixties, ready for its close-up, transforming into a kaleidoscope of sound, style, and spectacle. Let's twist and shout our way through Eurovision's swinging sixties.

The contest entered the '60s with a swagger, buoyed by growing popularity and an expanding list of participating countries. The decade began with a sense of optimism and a desire to showcase Europe's newfound stability and unity. However, behind the scenes, the contest faced growing pains. The increasing number of participants presented significant logistical and technical challenges. Coordinating multiple languages, managing different broadcasting standards, and ensuring fair voting procedures required international cooperation and innovative solutions. In 1961, Yugoslavia shattered the Iron Curtain's dominance, bringing Eastern European rhythms and melodies to the Eurovision stage. Their entry, performed in Serbo-Croatian, marked a pivotal moment, demonstrating the contest's potential to bridge cultural divides. However, their participation also sparked controversy, with some Western European countries expressing reservations about including a communist nation in this celebration of European unity. This tension highlighted the delicate political balance Eurovision had to navigate, even in its early years. Despite the initial apprehension, Yugoslavia's inclusion paved the way for future participation from Eastern European countries, enriching the contest's musical and cultural landscape.

The contest itself was evolving rapidly. Gone were the simple staging and demure performances of the 1950s. This was the decade that unleashed wind machines, elaborate costumes, and enough hairspray to deplete the ozone layer. The arrival of color television in 1968 revolutionized the viewing experience. Suddenly, viewers at home could fully appreciate the dazzling (and sometimes garish) costumes that were becoming a Eurovision trademark. Improved camera technology and sophisticated lighting designs transformed the contest into a visual spectacle, setting the stage for the elaborate productions of later decades. This shift towards a more visually driven contest mirrored the growing influence of television in popular culture, with audiences increasingly captivated by dynamic performances and eye-catching costumes. The '60s also saw the rise of fashion as a key element of Eurovision. Performances became a veritable catwalk, showcasing iconic (and sometimes questionable) styles, from bouffant hairdos and mini-skirts to bold geometric patterns and tailored suits. Specific examples include the iconic mini-dress worn by the UK's Sandie Shaw in 1967, a fashion statement that reflected the youthful energy of the era. Shaw's barefoot performance also subverted Eurovision norms. Other performers embraced the glamour of the decade with sequined gowns, feathered boas, and sharply tailored suits, creating memorable looks that captured the spirit of the swinging sixties.

The '60s delivered unforgettable musical moments. France Gall's "Poupée de cire, poupée de son" in 1965 wasn't just a winning song; it was a yé-yé revolution set to music, sparking controversy with its suggestive lyrics and cementing Serge Gainsbourg's reputation as Eurovision's enfant terrible. The song's success reflected a broader trend towards more contemporary and edgy pop music, challenging the dominance of traditional ballads in the contest. Udo Jürgens, representing Austria for three consecutive years (1964-1966), finally clinched the win on his third attempt with the heartfelt ballad "Merci, Chérie." His persistence set a precedent for future Eurovision hopefuls, demonstrating that sometimes, capturing the Eurovision crown requires more than one try. Perhaps no moment better encapsulates the delightful chaos of '60s Eurovision than the unprecedented four-way tie of 1969. France, Spain, the Netherlands, and the United Kingdom all shared the top spot, a result that sent shockwaves through the Eurovision community. This historic tie exposed a critical flaw in the voting system, where multiple countries could achieve the same maximum score.

The EBU, faced with this unprecedented situation, was forced to improvise, and the resulting confusion on stage became an instant Eurovision legend. The tie sparked heated debates about the fairness of the voting process and led to the introduction of a tie-breaker rule for subsequent contests. This change, implemented the following year, ensured that future contests would have a clear winner, even in the event of a tie at the top of the leaderboard. The 1969 tie remains a cautionary tale in Eurovision history, highlighting the need for a robust and adaptable voting system.

Amidst the evolving voting systems and growing international rivalries, a distinctive "Eurovision sound" began to emerge in the '60s. This sound, distinct from mainstream pop music of the time, was characterized by its catchy melodies, often dramatic key changes, and frequently multilingual lyrics. Winning songs like France Gall's "Poupée de cire, poupée de son" (1965), which blended catchy melodies with slightly risqué lyrics, and Sandie Shaw's "Puppet on a String" (1967), which had a more contemporary, upbeat sound despite its slightly darker undertones, exemplified this trend. Other notable entries, like Cliff Richard's 1968 entry, "Congratulations," further cemented the emergence of this distinctive style. Love it or hate it, the "Eurovision sound," a topic of passionate debate for decades, was here to stay. The '60s also saw Eurovision grapple with weightier issues, including censorship and political controversy. The 1964 contest, held in Copenhagen, was overshadowed by protests against Spain's Francisco Franco regime. This event demonstrated that even a song contest could become a platform for political expression, and highlighted the growing influence of Eurovision on Europe's social and political landscape. The language rule, requiring countries to perform in their national language, was also a source of debate. Some countries argued that singing in English would broaden their audience, while others prioritized preserving linguistic diversity. This debate, which would continue to resurface throughout Eurovision's history, reflected broader cultural and political tensions within Europe. Then there's the curious case of Domenico Modugno. His 1958 entry "Nel blu dipinto di blu" (better known as "Volare"), despite only placing third, went on to achieve international superstardom, winning two Grammy Awards and becoming one of the most recognizable songs of the 20th century. "Volare's" phenomenal success showcased Eurovision's growing influence and its ability to launch songs onto the global stage. It also sparked debates about how to define "Eurovision success"—should a song's impact be measured by global popularity or contest placement?

As Eurovision's popularity soared, so did its global reach. By the end of the decade, broadcasts extended far beyond Europe, captivating audiences from Australia to Canada. This international viewership added a new dimension to the contest, transforming it from a purely European affair into a global phenomenon. In Australia, for example, dedicated fan clubs emerged, organizing Eurovision viewing parties and celebrating European culture from afar. This early international following demonstrated Eurovision's ability to transcend geographical boundaries and connect people through shared musical experiences. As the '60s drew to a close, Eurovision stood at a crossroads. The contest had weathered the growing pains of expansion, faced technological challenges, navigated political controversies, and seen the emergence of a unique musical identity. It had transformed from a modest post-war experiment into a bona fide cultural phenomenon, ready to sashay into the 1970s with all the glitter, drama, and off-key charm it could muster. The stage was set for even greater spectacles to come, and a new era in entertainment history beckoned.

Eurovision Winners Of The 1960S

Year	Host City	Winner (Country)	Song Title
1960	London	Jacqueline Boyer (France)	Tom Pillibi
1961	Cannes	Jean-Claude Pascal (Luxembourg)	Nous les amoureux
1962	Luxembourg	Isabelle Aubret (France)	Un premier amour
1963	London	Grethe & Jørgen Ingmann (Denmark)	Dansevise
1964	Copenhagen	Gigliola Cinquetti (Italy)	Non ho l'età
1965	Naples	France Gall (Luxembourg)	Poupée de cire, poupée de son
1966	Luxembourg	Udo Jürgens (Austria)	Merci, Chérie
1967	Vienna	Sandie Shaw (United Kingdom)	Puppet on a String
1968	London	Massiel (Spain)	La, la, la...
1969	Madrid	Four-way tie: Frida Boccara (France)	Un jour, un enfant
		Lenny Kuhr (Netherlands)	De troubadour
		Lulu (United Kingdom)	Boom Bang-a-Bang
		Salomé (Spain)	Vivo cantando

Did You Know?

- In 1969, the voting system caused absolute chaos! There was a four-way tie for first place because, at the time, there was no tie-breaker rule. The EBU hurriedly introduced a tie-breaker rule the following year.
- The 1960 contest was the first Eurovision broadcast by the BBC in the UK. However, most of the footage of this contest is now sadly lost.
- Katie Boyle, who hosted the contest four times (1960, 1963, 1968, and 1974), holds the record for hosting the most Eurovision Song Contests.

CHAPTER 3: EUROVISION IN THE DISCO ERA (1970-1979)

Grab your flares, feather boas, and platform shoes, because we're about to boogie our way through Eurovision's disco decade! The 1970s were a time of glitter, glam, and some seriously questionable fashion choices. But beneath the sequins and the spectacle, the contest was evolving, grappling with issues of language, identity, and the rise of a certain Swedish supergroup that would change everything.

The contest entered the '70s with a swagger, buoyed by its growing popularity and an ever-expanding roster of participating countries. Malta shimmied onto the stage in 1971, and Israel broke new ground in 1973 as the first non-European country to participate. Suddenly, Eurovision was less "Euro" and more "vision" – a glimpse into a future where music could truly transcend borders, and perhaps even continents.

But it wasn't just the participant list that was expanding. The contest itself was evolving faster than you could say "disco inferno." Gone were the days of simple staging and demure performances. The '70s brought us glitter cannons, wind machines, and enough polyester to clothe a small nation. In 1975, Eurovision introduced its now-iconic "douze points" voting system, adding an extra layer of drama to the proceedings and giving rise to the time-honored tradition of complaining about political voting.

Speaking of politics, even as Eurovision tried to maintain its apolitical stance, the real world kept creeping in. Greece made its debut in 1974 following the fall of the military junta, while Turkey joined the party in 1975. Eurovision had become a debutante ball for fledgling democracies. The 1976 Greek entry even managed to sneak in a protest song about the Turkish invasion of Cyprus, proving that even in Eurovision, you can't escape geopolitics – you can only set it to a catchy tune. This increased the sense that even a song contest could be impacted by real world events.

But let's talk about the music, shall we? The '70s gave us some of Eurovision's most iconic performances, none more so than ABBA's triumph in 1974 with "Waterloo." The Swedish supergroup proved that Eurovision could be a launchpad for global stardom, and suddenly every participant was dreaming of becoming the next dancing queen (or king).

Other memorable winners included Brotherhood of Man's "Save Your Kisses for Me" in 1976, which became a global hit and probably soundtracked at least one of your parents' dates. And who could forget Israel's back-to-back disco-inspired wins in 1978 and 1979 with "A-Ba-Ni-Bi" and "Hallelujah"? It was as if the entire contest had been sprinkled with magical disco dust.

Behind the scenes, Eurovision was grappling with the challenges of its own success. Broadcasting a live event across an ever-growing number of countries was no small feat in the '70s. It required more technological wizardry than a Star Wars movie and more diplomacy than a UN summit. The introduction of satellite technology made it possible to beam the contest to an even wider audience, including viewers outside of Europe who were apparently eager to experience the unique combination of music, drama, and questionable fashion choices that only Eurovision could provide.

The language rule became a hot topic of debate during the '70s. From 1973 to 1976, countries were allowed to sing in any language they chose, leading to a surge in English-language entries. It was like Eurovision's own tower of Babel moment, only with better choreography. But in 1977, the national language restriction was reimposed, reportedly due to complaints from some countries that others were gaining an unfair advantage. Because nothing says "cultural unity" quite like arguing over which language you should sing in.

As Eurovision's popularity grew, so did its influence on the music industry. Winners often saw their songs become hits across the continent, and the "Eurovision sound" – a curious blend of catchy melodies, dramatic key changes, and lyrics that were often lost in translation – became a recognizable style in its own right. Eurovision became a musical melting pot, where traditional ballads could coexist with disco beats and the occasional yodeling interlude.

Fashion-wise, Eurovision in the '70s was a veritable catwalk of the decade's most iconic (and sometimes questionable) style choices. From ABBA's glam-rock inspired outfits to the flowing gowns and sharp suits of other contestants, the contest reflected and sometimes exaggerated the fashion trends of the era. It was a time when no outfit was too sparkly, no collar too wide, and no platform too high.

As the '70s drew to a close, Eurovision stood at a crossroads. It had transformed from a modest song contest into a bona fide cultural phenomenon. It had weathered changes in format, embraced new technologies, launched international careers, and even dipped its toes into political waters. But as the new decade dawned, one thing was clear: Eurovision was ready to face the '80s with all the glitter, drama, and off-key charm it could muster.

The Eurovision Song Contest had come of age in the disco era. It had found its groove, its style, and its place in the cultural landscape of Europe. As it moonwalked into the 1980s, Eurovision was more than just a song contest – it was a glittery, occasionally off-key, but always entertaining reflection of European pop culture. The stage was set for even greater spectacles to come. After all, in Eurovision, the show must always go on – preferably with more sequins than the year before.

Eurovision Winners Of The 1970S

Year	Host City	Winner (Country)	Song Title
1970	Amsterdam	Dana (Ireland)	All Kinds of Everything
1971	Dublin	Séverine (Monaco)	Un banc, un arbre, une rue
1972	Edinburgh	Vicky Leandros (Luxembourg)	Après Toi
1973	Luxembourg	Anne-Marie David (Luxembourg)	Tu te reconnaîtras
1974	Brighton	ABBA (Sweden)	Waterloo
1975	Stockholm	Teach-In (Netherlands)	Ding-a-dong
1976	The Hague	Brotherhood of Man (UK)	Save Your Kisses for Me
1977	London	Marie Myriam (France)	L'oiseau et l'enfant
1978	Paris	Izhar Cohen & the Alphabeta (Israel)	A-Ba-Ni-Bi
1979	Jerusalem	Milk and Honey (Israel)	Hallelujah

Did You Know?

- The 1974 contest in Brighton is often cited as one of the most-watched Eurovision Song Contests ever, with an estimated global audience of over 300 million viewers, thanks in no small part to a particular Swedish pop group.
- Brotherhood of Man's "Save Your Kisses for Me" (1976) was one of the rare Eurovision winners which gained popularity and became a chart hit before it entered the contest.
- The Dutch band Teach-In's "Ding-a-dong" became their only major hit despite a reasonably successful international career spanning multiple years and several albums.

CHAPTER 4: EUROVISION IN THE AGE OF NEW WAVE AND POWER BALLADS (1980-1989)

Synthesizers, shoulder pads, and enough hairspray to create a hole in the ozone layer – just another day at Eurovision in the 1980s! From big hair to even bigger power ballads, the contest fully embraced the decade's excess. It was a time of bold fashion statements, pioneering performances, and the rise of a certain Canadian diva who would conquer the world (one dramatic key change at a time).

The '80s dawned on a Europe still divided by the Iron Curtain, but united in its love for synthesizers and big hair. Eurovision, ever the cultural chameleon, was ready to adapt to the changing times faster than you could say "Video Killed the Radio Star."

Our plucky contest entered the decade with a bang – or rather, a brief foray into North Africa. Morocco made its first and only appearance in 1980, presumably deciding after one try that sequins and sand don't mix. Meanwhile, Cyprus shimmied onto the Eurovision stage in 1981, and Iceland broke the ice with its debut in 1986. The Eurovision family was growing, and like any good family, it was getting more complicated by the year.

But it wasn't just the participant list that was expanding. The contest itself was evolving faster than Madonna's fashion choices. The '80s saw Eurovision embrace new technologies with the enthusiasm of a teenager getting their first home computer. Suddenly, performances weren't just about the music – they were multimedia extravaganzas.

The influence of MTV and the rise of music videos was palpable. Acts were no longer content with standing still and belting out a tune. Oh no, now they needed elaborate staging, costume changes, and more special effects than a George Lucas film. The Eurovision stage became a playground for creative directors with fever dreams of dry ice and laser beams. This shift in performance style was a reflection of a broader change within the music industry, with music videos becoming more and more important.

Speaking of performances, the '80s gave us some of Eurovision's most iconic moments. Who could forget Bucks Fizz's skirt-ripping routine in 1981? Their performance of "Making Your Mind Up" had more layers than an onion and probably inspired a generation of wardrobe malfunctions. The UK group's victory proved that sometimes, in Eurovision, style could triumph over substance –

especially if that style involved tearaway clothing.

But it wasn't all gimmicks and velcro. The '80s also gave us some genuinely touching moments. In 1982, Germany's Nicole won hearts across the continent with "Ein bißchen Frieden" (A Little Peace), a song that resonated deeply in a Europe still shadowed by the Cold War. It was a reminder that beneath the glitz and glamour, Eurovision could still be a platform for messages of hope and unity.

And then there was Johnny Logan, the man who became known as "Mr. Eurovision." The Irish crooner pulled off the seemingly impossible feat of winning the contest twice as a performer – in 1980 with "What's Another Year" and again in 1987 with "Hold Me Now." Not content with this double victory, he went on to write Ireland's winning entry in 1992. Many wondered if Logan had cracked some secret Eurovision code and it left the rest of Europe wondering if Ireland had somehow found a four-leaf clover farm!

But perhaps the most surprising victory of the decade came in 1988, when a relatively unknown Canadian singer named Celine Dion took the crown for Switzerland with "Ne partez pas sans moi." It was a performance that launched a thousand power ballads – and one spectacular career. Who knew that Eurovision would be the launchpad for a voice that would go on to dominate '90s pop and make sure we'd never let go of that Titanic soundtrack?

Musically, the '80s were a time of great change for Eurovision. The disco beats of the '70s gave way to the synthesizer-heavy sounds of new wave and the soaring melodies of power ballads. It was as if the contest was trying to cram every '80s musical trend into three minutes or less. From the synth-pop stylings of Germany's Wind to the rock-tinged performances of Norway's Bobbysocks, Eurovision became a musical buffet where every taste was catered for – whether you wanted it or not.

Behind the scenes, Eurovision was grappling with the challenges of its own success. Broadcasting a live event across an ever-growing number of countries in the '80s required more technical wizardry than a NASA launch. The introduction of new sound and video technologies meant that each year's contest was bigger, louder, and more visually spectacular than the last. It was an arms race of entertainment, and nobody wanted to be left behind.

The role of the orchestra conductor became increasingly prominent during this decade. These unsung heroes, armed with only a baton and a dream, became featured parts of the performances. It was like watching a high-stakes game of musical charades, with conductors frantically trying to keep up with the increasingly complex arrangements. One wrong wave of the baton, and you could end up with a power ballad being played at disco tempo.

Politically, Eurovision in the '80s was like a glittery mirror held up to Europe. The contest continued to reflect the continent's divisions and alliances, even as it tried to maintain its apolitical stance. Israel's hosting of the contest in Jerusalem in 1979 (technically the '70s, but setting the stage for the '80s) and again in 1999 brought the Middle East conflict into sharp focus. Meanwhile, the ongoing Cold War meant that Eastern Bloc countries were still conspicuously absent from the Eurovision stage.

The language rule continued to be a hot topic of debate. The national language restriction remained in place, leading to some creative interpretations. Belgium, in particular, took advantage of its multilingual status to perform in a different language each year. It was like linguistic roulette – you never knew whether you'd be getting French, Dutch, or possibly even interpretive dance.

Commercially, Eurovision continued to launch careers and produce hit songs. While not every winner went on to ABBA-level success, many found fame beyond the contest. Germany's Nicole, Bucks Fizz, and of course, Celine Dion all parlayed their Eurovision victories into successful careers. The "Eurovision sound" became a recognizable style in its own right, influencing pop music across the continent. Eurovision had become a hit factory, churning out catchy tunes and potential stars faster than you could say "douze points."

Fashion-wise, the '80s were a time when no shoulder pad was too big, no hairstyle too gravity-defying, and no outfit too garish for the Eurovision stage. It was a decade that asked, "Can you ever have too much of a good thing?" and answered with a resounding "No!" From Bucks Fizz's iconic skirt-ripping outfits to the parade of puffy sleeves, leather pants, and enough sparkles to blind a satellite, Eurovision in the '80s was a fashion show like no other.

The '80s also saw its fair share of controversies and memorable moments. The dreaded "nul points" became a more frequent occurrence, with an unprecedented three songs receiving zero points in 1983. It was a stark reminder that in Eurovision, you could go from hero to zero faster than you could change a synthesizer preset.

As the decade drew to a close, Eurovision stood on the brink of a new era. The Berlin Wall was about to fall, bringing with it the promise of a new, united Europe. The contest had weathered the storm of '80s excess, embraced new technologies, and somehow managed to keep its sequins on straight through it all.

The Eurovision Song Contest had ridden the new wave and belted out its fair share of power ballads. It had found its voice (sometimes autotuned), its style (often questionable), and its place in the cultural landscape of Europe. As it prepared to moonwalk into the 1990s, Eurovision was more than just a song contest – it was a glittery, occasionally off-key, but always entertaining reflection of European pop culture.

The stage was set for even greater spectacles to come. After all, in Eurovision, the show must always go on – preferably with more key changes than the decade before. The '90s were calling, and Eurovision was ready to answer – just as soon as it finished teasing its hair and adjusting its shoulder pads.

Eurovision Winners Of The 1980S

Year	Host City	Winner (Country)	Song Title
1980	The Hague	Johnny Logan (Ireland)	What's Another Year
1981	Dublin	Bucks Fizz (United Kingdom)	Making Your Mind Up
1982	Harrogate	Nicole (Germany)	Ein bißchen Frieden
1983	Munich	Corinne Hermès (Luxembourg)	Si la vie est cadeau
1984	Luxembourg	Herreys (Sweden)	Diggi-Loo Diggi-Ley
1985	Gothenburg	Bobbysocks! (Norway)	La det swinge
1986	Bergen	Sandra Kim (Belgium)	J'aime la vie
1987	Brussels	Johnny Logan (Ireland)	Hold Me Now
1988	Dublin	Céline Dion (Switzerland)	Ne partez pas sans moi
1989	Lausanne	Riva (Yugoslavia)	Rock Me

Did You Know?

- The 1981 contest in Dublin featured a striking stage design that included a real waterfall. However, it wasn't without its problems – the waterfall caused some technical issues during the live show.

- Luxembourg's 1983 winning song, "Si la vie est cadeau," was nearly disqualified because parts of it had been previously performed.

- Sandra Kim, the winner for Belgium in 1986 with "J'aime la vie," was only 13 years old at the time, making her the youngest-ever Eurovision winner. This prompted the introduction of an age restriction in the next few years.

CHAPTER 5: EUROVISION IN THE POST-COLD WAR ERA (1990-1999)

Walls were crumbling, borders were shifting, and Eurovision was about to get a whole lot bigger. The 1990s ushered in a new era for the contest, one defined by geopolitical change, musical experimentation, and an influx of new nations eager to make their mark on the European stage. From power ballads to techno beats, the contest became a melting pot of cultures, styles, and enough key changes to make your head spin.

The fall of the Berlin Wall and the Iron Curtain didn't just reshape Europe's political landscape; it gave Eurovision a whole new guest list. Suddenly, the contest was facing an identity crisis bigger than a teenager in a boy band. Was it ready to transform from a cozy Western European shindig into a pan-European extravaganza? Spoiler alert: It was about to find out.

As the decade kicked off, Eurovision found itself in a position not unlike a host who'd sent out too many party invitations. The influx of new participating countries, particularly from the former Soviet and Yugoslav republics, turned the contest into the musical equivalent of a game of Tetris. How many countries could they squeeze in before the whole thing toppled over?

This explosion of participants led to one of the most significant changes in Eurovision history: the introduction of qualification rounds. Eurovision had suddenly developed a VIP list, complete with velvet rope and clipboard-wielding bouncers. Countries now had to earn their spot in the grand final, leading to a new layer of drama and disappointment. Nothing says "welcome to Europe" quite like being told you didn't make the cut for a singing contest.

The voting system, too, got a makeover. The '90s saw experiments with different voting methods faster than you could say "douze points." It does feel like the organisers were (and still are) determined to find the perfect mathematical formula for measuring the unmeasurable: musical taste across an entire continent.

Technologically, Eurovision in the '90s was like a teenager getting their first computer. The contest embraced new technologies with the enthusiasm of a dad with a new camcorder. The live orchestra, once as much a part of Eurovision as key changes and wind machines, began its swan song. By the end of the decade, it had been replaced by backing tracks, much to the chagrin of purists and the delight of budget-conscious producers everywhere.

Computer graphics made their debut, turning the Eurovision stage into something resembling a Windows 95 screensaver. It was a brave new world of visual effects, where no performance was complete without a dizzying array of swirling graphics that looked like they'd been designed by a toddler with a new box of crayons.

But let's talk about the music, shall we? The '90s gave us some of Eurovision's most iconic performances, none more so than Ireland's domination in the early part of the decade. The Emerald Isle won four times in five years, leading many to suspect they'd found a secret leprechaun gold mine of musical talent. Or perhaps they'd just mastered the art of the Eurovision power ballad, a skill more valuable than any pot of gold in this contest.

Speaking of Ireland, we can't discuss '90s Eurovision without mentioning Riverdance. This interval act from the 1994 contest in Dublin went on to become a global phenomenon, proving that sometimes the filler can be more memorable than the main event. It was as if all those years of Irish contestants standing still and belting out ballads had created a pent-up energy that exploded in a fury of synchronized tap dancing.

The '90s also saw Eurovision continue its tradition of launching international careers. Katrina and the Waves brought a ray of sunshine to the UK's Eurovision fortunes in 1997 with "Love Shine a Light." It was a rare moment of Eurovision glory for the Brits in a decade that saw their fortunes wane faster than you could say "nul points."

A pivotal moment that solidified Eurovision's reputation as a champion of social progress arrived in 1998. Dana International, a transgender woman representing Israel, secured a groundbreaking victory with her song "Diva." This win wasn't solely about musical talent; it was a cultural earthquake that shattered taboos and catapulted LGBTQ+ visibility onto an international stage. Dana's triumph transcended the competition, sparking intense debates across Europe and beyond about gender identity, acceptance, and the evolving role of the Eurovision Song Contest. While the contest had always enjoyed a degree of camp and a strong following in the LGBTQ+ community, Dana's win marked an explicit embrace of diversity and a powerful statement against discrimination.

Musically, the '90s were a time of great diversity for Eurovision. The contest became a melting pot of styles, where pop rubbed shoulders with rock, and ethnic sounds blended with electronic beats. It was like a musical buffet where you could sample a little bit of everything, from Swedish schlager to Croatian rap. The power ballad, of course, remained a Eurovision staple. After all, why sing when you can belt, and why have one key change when you can have three?

In the 1990s, Eurovision mirrored the political transformation of Europe. The collapse of the Soviet Union and Yugoslavia brought a wave of new countries to the contest, all eager to establish their presence on the European stage. For many viewers, Eurovision became a rapid lesson in the shifting European geography, as they struggled to locate unfamiliar countries on a map.

This influx of new nations also gave rise to the phenomenon of voting blocs and neighborly voting patterns. Suddenly, it wasn't just about the music – it was about geopolitics, shared cultural ties, and possibly a few under-the-table deals involving surplus vegetables and promises of future tourism campaigns.

Eurovision voting became a subject worthy of doctoral theses, with commentators analyzing every "douze points" as if it held the secret to world peace.

For many of these new countries, Eurovision became a platform for national branding. It was their chance to say to Europe, "Hey, we exist, we have culture, and we can sing... sort of." Some embraced their folk traditions, others went full-on pop, and a brave few decided that what Europe really needed was a rap song about the socio-economic challenges of post-Soviet states (looking at you, Lithuania 1994).

The language rule continued to be a hot topic of debate throughout the decade. The restriction to national languages remained in place for most of the '90s, leading to some creative interpretations and a few performances that sounded like they were being sung in Klingon. But in 1999, the free language rule was reintroduced, opening the floodgates for a tsunami of English-language pop songs.

The 1990s witnessed a shift in the commercial landscape of the Eurovision Song Contest. While the decade didn't replicate the global phenomenon of ABBA in the 1970s, it still yielded notable successes. Ireland's Niamh Kavanagh, the 1993 winner with "In Your Eyes," not only achieved widespread recognition but also secured the top position on charts across Europe, proving that Eurovision could still generate commercially successful hits.

However, the contest's influence on European pop music was undergoing a transformation. The era when a Eurovision victory guaranteed pan-European stardom was fading. The 1990s music scene was a diverse landscape with competing genres like grunge,

Britpop, and boy bands, each vying for dominance. Eurovision found itself navigating a unique position—still capable of launching careers, as evidenced by acts like Niamh Kavanagh, but increasingly perceived as an unconventional counterpart to mainstream pop. This period also saw the rise of power ballads and ethnic-inspired entries, reflecting the evolving musical trends of the decade. Despite the shifting dynamics, Eurovision's enduring appeal and ability to surprise and entertain audiences remained undeniable, solidifying its position as a beloved cultural institution in Europe and beyond.

The Eurovision Song Contest underwent a significant transformation behind the scenes during the 1990s. The decision to phase out the live orchestra marked a turning point in the contest's production. The sight of conductors passionately guiding their musicians through intricate scores, their batons a blur as they navigated the crescendos and key changes, became a relic of the past. In its place, pre-recorded backing tracks took centre stage. While this shift undeniably led to performances that were slicker and more technically precise, it also sacrificed some of the raw energy and spontaneity that live music brought to the contest. The move to backing tracks symbolised a broader shift towards a more polished and predictable Eurovision, where meticulous studio production often overshadowed the unpredictable magic of live performance.

Notable hosts of the decade included Ireland's Mary Kennedy, who had the unenviable task of hosting the contest three years in a row. One can only imagine the sense of déjà vu as she welcomed Europe to Dublin year after year. For a period in the 1990's it was as if Ireland had a timeshare on the Eurovision stage, and they were determined to get their money's worth.

Fashion in '90s Eurovision was a spectacle unto itself. The decade that brought us grunge and minimalism seemed to have passed Eurovision by entirely. Instead, the contest embraced an aesthetic that can only be described as "more is more." Shoulder pads continued their reign of terror, joined by an army of sequins, feathers, and enough leather to make a herd of cows nervous. It often looked like every performer had raided the wardrobe department of a sci-fi B-movie and then added glitter.

The '90s also had its fair share of controversies and memorable moments. Norway's "nul points" in 1997 proved that even in a decade of change, some traditions remained sacred. The Norwegian entry, "San Francisco," failed to score a single point, joining the exclusive (and probably not very fun) "nul points" club. It was a reminder that in Eurovision, you're never too far from glory – or utter humiliation.

Eurovision's global reach continued to expand throughout the decade. The contest found eager audiences in Australia, where it aired in the wee hours of the morning, creating a tradition of Eurovision parties that rivaled any in Europe. It seemed that the appeal of watching Europeans make fools of themselves on stage transcended time zones and continents.

As the millennium approached, Eurovision stood at a crossroads. The contest had transformed from a cozy Western European affair into a pan-European extravaganza. It had weathered the storms of geopolitical change, embraced new technologies (sometimes reluctantly), and somehow managed to keep its sequins on straight through it all.

The Eurovision Song Contest of the '90s was a reflection of a continent in flux. It had found its voice (sometimes autotuned), its style (often questionable), and its place in the cultural landscape of a new Europe. As it prepared to strut into the new millennium, Eurovision was more than just a song contest – it was a glittery, occasionally off-key, but always entertaining barometer of European unity and diversity.

The stage was set for even greater spectacles to come. After all, in Eurovision, the show must always go on – preferably with more wind machines, more pyrotechnics, and at least one song about cyber-love in the digital age. The 2000s were calling, and Eurovision was ready to answer – just as soon as it finished applying one last layer of glitter.

As we bid farewell to the '90s, we can't help but marvel at how far Eurovision had come. From its humble post-war beginnings to this sprawling, sparkling celebration of European music and culture, the contest had proven itself as adaptable as a Swedish pop song and as resilient as a diva's hairspray. The '90s may have been over, but for Eurovision, the party was just getting started. Bring on the new millennium – douze points all around!

Eurovision Winners Of The 1990S

Year	Host City	Winner (Country)	Song Title
1990	Zagreb	Toto Cutugno (Italy)	Insieme: 1992
1991	Rome	Carola (Sweden)	Fångad av en stormvind
1992	Malmö	Linda Martin (Ireland)	Why Me?
1993	Millstreet	Niamh Kavanagh (Ireland)	In Your Eyes
1994	Dublin	Paul Harrington & Charlie McGettigan (Ireland)	Rock 'n' Roll Kids
1995	Dublin	Secret Garden (Norway)	Nocturne
1996	Oslo	Eimear Quinn (Ireland)	The Voice
1997	Dublin	Katrina and the Waves (United Kingdom)	Love Shine a Light
1998	Birmingham	Dana International (Israel)	Diva
1999	Jerusalem	Charlotte Nilsson (Sweden)	Take Me to Your Heaven

Did You Know?

- The 1994 contest is famous for launching the international phenomenon Riverdance during the interval act. Composed by Bill Whelan, the performance captivated audiences worldwide and spawned a hugely successful stage show.

- In 1997, Katrina and the Waves achieved something rare for the UK in the contest at this point: winning! "Love Shine a Light" became a huge hit and marked the last time the UK actually claimed first place for the next 26 years.

- In a twist of Eurovision fate, Norway's "nul points" in 1997, with their entry "San Francisco," was particularly noteworthy as it was only two years after their last win in 1995 with "Nocturne." It goes to show that Eurovision results can change very quickly.

CHAPTER 6: EUROVISION IN THE NEW MILLENNIUM (2000-2009)

As the world partied like it was 1999 (and survived Y2K), Eurovision sashayed into the new millennium, ready to embrace the digital age. The noughties were a time of technological innovation, musical fusion, and the rise of some seriously catchy tunes. From monster masks to heartfelt ballads, the contest continued to surprise, delight, and occasionally bewilder us.

Europe, fresh from its millennial hangover, found itself in a brave new world of Nokia phones, Britney Spears, and the dawn of reality TV. Eurovision, never one to be left behind (unless it was fashionably so), was ready to evolve faster than you could say "Flying the flag for you."

The contest entered the new millennium like an eager teenager with a new MySpace account – ready to make friends, push boundaries, and occasionally make a fool of itself. The influx of new participating countries continued, turning Eurovision into a geopolitical jigsaw puzzle where the pieces were made of glitter and held together by power ballads.

But with great expansion came great logistical nightmares. By 2004, Eurovision had more wannabe participants than a casting call for "European Idol." The solution? The introduction of the semi-final system. Suddenly, Eurovision became a two-night extravaganza, with countries battling it out for a spot in the grand final. It was a huge change for the competition, adding a new element of drama to the proceedings.

The voting system, too, got a millennial makeover. Televoting, introduced in the late '90s, became the norm, giving viewers at home the power to shape Eurovision destiny. It was democracy in action – if your definition of democracy involved voting for the country with the best wind machine usage. Later in the decade, a combined jury/televoting system was introduced, in an attempt to balance popular appeal with musical merit. Because nothing says "artistic integrity" quite like a panel of experts judging a man dressed as a giant turkey singing about world peace.

Technologically, Eurovision in the 2000s was like a teenager discovering social media for the first time. The rise of platforms like Facebook and YouTube gave fans new ways to obsess over their favorite acts, dissect every performance, and argue endlessly about whether that key change was really necessary (spoiler alert: it always is in Eurovision).

The staging and special effects reached new heights of extravagance. Gone were the days when a couple of sparklers and a wind machine could impress. Now, if your performance didn't involve pyrotechnics, complex choreography, and enough flashing lights to trigger a seizure warning, were you even trying?

But let's talk about the music, shall we? The 2000s gave us some of Eurovision's most iconic performances, none more so than Lordi's hard rock victory for Finland in 2006. It was as if Eurovision had looked at its image of cheesy pop and sugary ballads and decided, "You know what this needs? Monster masks and electric guitars." Finland's win proved that in Eurovision, sometimes the way to stand out is to scare the living daylights out of everyone.

Estonia made history in 2001 as the first former Soviet country to win the contest. Tanel Padar, Dave Benton & 2XL's "Everybody" had everybody dancing and marked a shift in the contest's centre of gravity eastward. Perhaps audiences were saying, "Western Europe, you've had your fun. Now let's see what the new kids on the bloc can do."

Russia, not to be outdone, clinched its first victory in 2008 with Dima Bilan's "Believe." The performance, which featured Olympic figure skater Evgeni Plushenko on a miniature ice rink, was peak Eurovision excess. Russia decided to showcase every talent they had in one go, just short of having a bear play the balalaika.

Musically, the 2000s were a time of great diversity for Eurovision. Pop still reigned supreme, but rock made a comeback, ethnic sounds fused with modern beats, and the "Eurovision sound" evolved into something that could only be described as "everything but the kitchen sink" (and sometimes, even that made an appearance as a percussion instrument).

The political dimension of Eurovision reached new heights in the

2000s. Voting blocs became the hot topic, with commentators analyzing every "douze points" as if it held the secret to solving the EU's agricultural policy. The expansion of the EU seemed to mirror Eurovision's own growth, leading to jokes about which was the real pan-European institution.

Some countries used Eurovision as a platform for social and political messages. Ukraine's 2004 entry, "Wild Dances" by Ruslana, became an anthem for the country's Orange Revolution. It was a powerful reminder that sometimes, a song contest could be about more than just music – it could be a voice for change, albeit one accompanied by a lot of leather and clanging jewelry.

The dominance of English-language songs in the contest continued to be a talking point. Between 2001 and 2008, six winning songs were performed entirely in English, even when it wasn't the representing country's national language. However, the later 2000s saw a resurgence of entries in national and even minority languages, as countries sought to showcase their unique cultural identities. This was exemplified by Serbia's 2007 win with "Molitva," performed entirely in Serbian, and Finland's 2006 entry, "Hard Rock Hallelujah," which included lyrics in both Finnish and English.

The Eurovision Song Contest's commercial impact in the noughties was significant, even if it didn't produce another global phenomenon like ABBA. The contest still left an indelible mark on the European music scene, with winners like Alexander Rybak, whose "Fairytale" for Norway in 2009 shattered records, finding success beyond the Eurovision stage. It seemed that, at least occasionally, Eurovision was transforming into a launching pad for careers that could extend far beyond the three minutes allocated for each song.

Behind the scenes, Eurovision was evolving faster than a boyband's dance routine. The production values skyrocketed, turning each contest into a spectacle that would make even the Super Bowl halftime show blush. Hosts were no longer just pretty faces reading from cue cards; they became multitasking marvels, expected to sing, dance, and possibly juggle flaming batons while introducing the next act from Moldova.

The decade saw a beloved Eurovision figure hang up his glittery microphone. Terry Wogan's dry humor and playful mockery of the often bizarre Eurovision entries made him a beloved figure in British television, and synonymous with the Eurovision Song Contest in the United Kingdom. His sardonic and witty commentary provided viewers at home with a unique and entertaining perspective, turning Eurovision watching into a sport where eye-rolling was an Olympic event. Wogan served as the UK's commentator for an impressive 35 years, from 1971 to 2008. His resignation in 2008 marked the end of an era, leaving fans wondering if anyone could ever match his level of delightful disdain.

Fashion in the 2000s Eurovision was a spectacle unto itself. The decade that brought us low-rise jeans and Ugg boots seemed to have inspired Eurovision designers to ask, "How can we make this more... extra?" Costume choices ranged from the sublime to the ridiculous, often within the same performance. Who could forget Ukraine's Verka Serduchka in 2007, dressed as a disco ball's fever dream? As ever, Eurovision had looked at conventional fashion and decided, "Nah, let's make our own rules."

The waving of Syrian flags by the Israeli participants during the 2000 Eurovision Song Contest was a spontaneous gesture of goodwill. The aim was to express a desire for peace and unity between the two countries, who have a long history of conflict. Although brief, the gesture was a powerful symbol of hope and a reminder that music can transcend political boundaries.

The act was widely seen as positive, but it also sparked some controversy. Some Israelis criticized the gesture as inappropriate given the ongoing tensions between the two countries. Others praised it as a brave step towards reconciliation. There was no official response from the Syrian government, but the act was widely discussed in the Syrian media. Some commentators expressed support for the gesture; others dismissed it as a publicity stunt.

Ukraine's 2005 victory with Ruslana's "Wild Dances" became intertwined with the country's Orange Revolution, showing that sometimes, a Eurovision song could become more than just a catchy tune – it could become a political anthem. Who knew that leather, whips, and tribal rhythms could be the soundtrack to democratic change?

Eurovision's global reach continued to expand throughout the decade. The contest found particularly fertile ground in Australia, where dedicated fans would wake up at ungodly hours to watch the spectacle live. It seemed that the appeal of watching Europeans make fools of themselves on stage transcended time zones and continents. Little did we know that this Aussie obsession would lead to even more surprising developments in the following decade.

As the 2000s drew to a close, Eurovision faced new challenges. The 2008 financial crisis left its mark on the contest, with some countries struggling to foot the bill for participation. It was a stark reminder that even in the glittery world of Eurovision, real-world problems could still intrude.

Looking back, the Eurovision Song Contest of the 2000s was a reflection of a continent – and a world – in flux. It had embraced the digital age, expanded its borders, and somehow managed to become even more outrageous in the process. As it prepared to strut into the 2010s, Eurovision was more than just a song contest – it was a glittery, occasionally off-key, but always entertaining barometer of European pop culture.

The stage was set for even greater spectacles to come. After all, in Eurovision, the show must always go on – preferably with more pyrotechnics, more outlandish costumes, and at least one performance that leaves viewers wondering, "Did that really just happen?" The 2010s were calling, and Eurovision was ready to answer – just as soon as it finished applying one last layer of glitter and practicing its final key change.

As we bid farewell to the noughties, we can't help but marvel at how far Eurovision had come. From its humble post-war beginnings to this sprawling, sparkling celebration of European music and culture, the contest had proven itself as adaptable as a Swedish pop song and as resilient as a diva's hairspray. The 2000s may have been over, but for Eurovision, the party was just getting started.

Eurovision Winners Of The 2000S

Year	Host City	Winner (Country)	Song Title
2000	Stockholm	Olsen Brothers (Denmark)	Fly on the Wings of Love
2001	Copenhagen	Tanel Padar, Dave Benton & 2XL (Estonia)	Everybody
2002	Tallinn	Marie N (Latvia)	I Wanna
2003	Riga	Sertab Erener (Turkey)	Everyway That I Can
2004	Istanbul	Ruslana (Ukraine)	Wild Dances
2005	Kyiv	Helena Paparizou (Greece)	My Number One
2006	Athens	Lordi (Finland)	Hard Rock Hallelujah
2007	Helsinki	Marija Šerifović (Serbia)	Molitva
2008	Belgrade	Dima Bilan (Russia)	Believe
2009	Moscow	Alexander Rybak (Norway)	Fairytale

Did You Know?

- The Olsen Brothers, who won for Denmark in 2000 with "Fly on the Wings of Love," were the oldest duo ever to win the contest at the time, with a combined age of 94.

- In 2004, Ukraine's Ruslana, with her high-energy performance of "Wild Dances," became a symbol of the Orange Revolution, a series of protests that took place in Ukraine following a disputed presidential election.

- Alexander Rybak's "Fairytale," representing Norway in 2009, achieved the highest-ever points total under the old voting system. It set a winning benchmark.

CHAPTER 7: EUROVISION IN THE AGE OF SOCIAL MEDIA (2010-2019)

Tweet this: Eurovision enters the 2010s, ready to slay, hashtag-ready, and more fabulous than ever! #EurovisionEvolution

As the world became obsessed with hashtags, selfies, and avocado toast, Eurovision strutted into the 2010s like it was walking the digital runway. Gone were the days when a simple wind machine and a key change could guarantee success. Now, if your performance wasn't trending on Twitter faster than a cat video, were you even trying?

The decade kicked off with Germany's Lena Meyer-Landrut charming Europe with "Satellite," a win that proved you didn't need pyrotechnics or elaborate staging to capture hearts. All you needed was a catchy tune, a quirky personality, and enough charisma to make even the most stoic Scandinavian crack a smile.

But let's rewind a bit. The 2010s saw Eurovision evolve faster than a teenager's Instagram feed. The "Big Five" rule was firmly established, guaranteeing France, Germany, Italy, Spain, and the UK a spot in the final with other countries competing to qualify through earlier rounds.

Next we saw the biggest, or perhaps furthest, stretching of the "Euro" term. Initially invited as a special guest to commemorate Eurovision's 60th anniversary in 2015, Australia's participation was meant to be a one-time affair. However, the Aussies embraced the contest with such enthusiasm and their vibrant performances resonated so strongly with audiences that their presence became a delightful fixture.

This unexpected development showcased Eurovision's ability to transcend geographical boundaries and embrace a truly global audience. Australia's continued participation underscored the contest's universal appeal and its capacity to foster connections across continents. What began as a celebratory gesture transformed into a symbol of Eurovision's inclusive spirit and its willingness to expand its horizons.

Technologically, Eurovision in the 2010s was like your grandpa discovering Snapchat filters. Suddenly, everything was interactive. The official Eurovision app allowed fans to vote, play along, and virtually experience what it's like to be a Swedish pop star (minus the perfect hair and impeccable fashion sense).

Staging reached new heights of extravagance. LED screens the size of small countries became the norm, turning performances into visual feasts that would make even James Cameron jealous. It was a far cry from the days when a couple of backup dancers and a sparkly outfit were considered cutting-edge.

But let's talk about the music, shall we? The 2010s gave us some of Eurovision's most iconic performances. Conchita Wurst's victory for Austria in 2014 with "Rise Like a Phoenix" was more than just a win; it was a cultural moment. Bearded drag queens had officially entered the mainstream, and Eurovision was leading the charge. Take that, conservative Europe!

Portugal's Salvador Sobral brought a different kind of revolution in 2017. His jazz-infused "Amar Pelos Dois" proved that sometimes, less is more. No fancy staging, no pyrotechnics, just pure emotion and musicality. For one year at least, Eurovision had suddenly remembered it was supposed to be a song contest.

The decade also saw its fair share of non-winning performances that captured the public's imagination. Who could forget Ukraine's Verka Serduchka in 2007 (okay, technically not this decade, but her legacy lived on) or Moldova's Epic Sax Guy in 2010? These moments proved that in Eurovision, sometimes coming seventh is better than winning, especially if you become a meme in the process.

Musically, the 2010s were a rollercoaster of trends. EDM and contemporary pop dominated the early part of the decade, with enough drops to make your average dubstep fan dizzy. But as the years went on, there was a return to authenticity. Suddenly, real instruments were cool again.

The political dimension of Eurovision reached new heights in the 2010s. LGBTQ+ representation became more prominent, with the contest embracing its status as a gay icon. Conchita Wurst's victory was just the tip of the fabulous iceberg. Geopolitical tensions also found their way onto the Eurovision stage, and the Russia-Ukraine conflict spilled over into the contest, culminating in Ukraine's ban of the Russian participant in 2017. It was a stark reminder that even in the glittery world of Eurovision, real-world problems could still intrude.

As for language, English continued its dominance, but there was a resurgence of native languages too. Perhaps countries had collectively realised that singing in English didn't guarantee success, so they might as well embrace their linguistic roots. After all, nothing says "cultural identity" quite like a power ballad in Montenegrin.

And so, as we pause halfway through this decade of digital transformation, it's clear that Eurovision in the 2010s was undergoing a metamorphosis as dramatic as any of its onstage costume reveals. The contest was growing up, reaching out, and occasionally going viral in the process.

Stay tuned for more social media shenanigans, fashion faux pas, and enough Europop to fill a decade's worth of Spotify playlists. After all, in Eurovision, the show must always go on – preferably with a trending hashtag.

Now, let's talk fashion, darlings. Eurovision in the 2010s was serving looks fiercer than a "RuPaul's Drag Race" finale. Gone were the days of simple sequined dresses and boring suits. Now, if your outfit couldn't double as modern art or potentially signal aliens, were you even trying? Moldova's Sunstroke Project returned in 2017 with enough tinfoil on their shoulders to contact extraterrestrial life. Meanwhile, Ukraine's Jamala in 2016 wore a dress that looked like it was designed by Mother Nature herself after a wild night out.

Behind the scenes, Eurovision had become more complex than a Scandinavian crime drama. Hosting the event was no longer just about having a nice venue and decent catering. Cities battled it out "Hunger Games" style for the honor, promising everything short of renaming their country "Eurovisia" to win the bid. The production values skyrocketed faster than a helium balloon at a children's party, turning each contest into a spectacle that would make even the Olympic opening ceremonies say, "Okay, maybe tone it down a notch?"

But darling, we simply must dish about the drama. The 2010s served up more controversy than a season of "Real Housewives of Eurovision" (note to TV producers: make this happen). Azerbaijan found itself in hot water in 2013 over alleged vote-buying. Apparently, someone forgot to tell them that "douze points" aren't actually for sale on Amazon.

And who could forget the great Madonna debacle of 2019? The Queen of Pop graced the Eurovision stage in Tel Aviv, delivering a performance that was more off-key than a piano in a hurricane. It was a moment that united Europe in collective cringe, proving that even global superstars can fall victim to the Eurovision curse.

Speaking of global, Eurovision's reach in the 2010s expanded faster than your waistline at a Swedish smörgåsbord. Eurovision parties popped up everywhere from Sydney to San Francisco. It seemed the whole world wanted a piece of the glittery pie. Fans in non-participating countries gathered at ungodly hours, dressed in more flags than the United Nations headquarters, ready to experience the joy, the drama, and the occasional "what on earth am I watching?" moments that only Eurovision can provide.

As the decade drew to a close, Eurovision faced new challenges. The rise of music streaming had changed the game faster than you could say "Spotify playlist." Suddenly, success wasn't just about winning on the night, but about how many streams you could rack up in the following weeks.

Looking back, the Eurovision Song Contest of the 2010s was a glitter-covered mirror held up to a rapidly changing world. It had embraced the digital age, expanded its borders, and somehow managed to become even more outrageous in the process. As it prepared to sashay into the 2020s, Eurovision was more than just a song contest – it was a global phenomenon, a celebration of diversity, and a reminder that no matter how divided the world might seem, we can always unite in our love of a good key change and a wind machine.

The stage was set for even greater spectacles to come. After all, in Eurovision, the show must always go on – preferably with more pyrotechnics, more outlandish costumes, and at least one performance that leaves viewers wondering, "Is this the fever dream of a glitter-addicted unicorn?" The 2020s were calling, and Eurovision was ready to answer – right after it finished updating its Instagram story.

Again, it was easy to marvel at how far Eurovision had come. From a quaint song contest to a global extravaganza that was part music competition, part fashion show, and part unintentional comedy – Eurovision had proven itself to be as enduring as a glitter stain on a white carpet. The 2010s may have been over, but for Eurovision, the party was just getting started. Bring on the next decade – may it be filled with more key changes, wind machines, and inexplicable prop choices than ever before!

Eurovision Winners Of The 2010S

Year	Host City	Winner (Country)	Song Title
2010	Oslo	Lena (Germany)	Satellite
2011	Düsseldorf	Ell & Nikki (Azerbaijan)	Running Scared
2012	Baku	Loreen (Sweden)	Euphoria
2013	Malmö	Emmelie de Forest (Denmark)	Only Teardrops
2014	Copenhagen	Conchita Wurst (Austria)	Rise Like a Phoenix
2015	Vienna	Måns Zelmerlöw (Sweden)	Heroes
2016	Stockholm	Jamala (Ukraine)	1944
2017	Kyiv	Salvador Sobral (Portugal)	Amar pelos dois
2018	Lisbon	Netta (Israel)	Toy
2019	Tel Aviv	Duncan Laurence (Netherlands)	Arcade

Did You Know?

- The "Big Five" rule, guaranteeing automatic qualification, wasn't universally popular. Some smaller countries argued it gave an unfair advantage, sparking debate about fairness and representation in the contest.
- Although it was hugely popular online and with fans, "Epic Sax Guy" (Moldova, 2010) only finished 22nd in the contest, proving that online popularity doesn't always translate to Eurovision success.
- In 2017, Portugal's Salvador Sobral won with "Amar pelos dois," a song performed entirely in Portuguese – the first time a winning song hadn't included any English lyrics since 1996. This win was seen as a triumph for musical authenticity in a contest often dominated by English-language pop.

CHAPTER 8: EUROVISION IN THE PANDEMIC ERA AND BEYOND (2020-PRESENT)

J ust when we thought Eurovision had seen it all – from ABBA's platform boots to Lordi's monster masks – along came a plot twist that not even the most dramatic key change could have prepared us for. Ladies and gentlemen, welcome to Eurovision in the time of COVID-19, where face masks became more essential than sequins, and social distancing meant keeping your wind machines at least two meters apart.

As 2020 dawned, Rotterdam was gearing up to host the 65th Eurovision Song Contest. The Dutch were ready to party like it was 1975 (the last time they'd hosted), and 41 countries were polishing their acts to within an inch of their glittery lives. But faster than you could say "douze points," a microscopic party pooper named COVID-19 gate-crashed Europe's biggest musical shindig.

On March 18, 2020, the unthinkable happened. For the first time in its 64-year history, Eurovision was cancelled. It was as if someone had unplugged Europe's karaoke machine and stolen all the glitter. Fans were left in shock, artists in limbo, and an entire continent wondering what they were going to do with their Saturday night in May.

The European Broadcasting Union (EBU) didn't make this decision lightly. They'd explored every possible alternative, from hosting without an audience (Eurovision without screaming fans? Sacrilege!) to remote performances (can you imagine the lag on the Estonian performance?). But as COVID-19 swept across Europe faster than a Swedish pop chorus, it became clear that the show simply couldn't go on.

But darlings, this is Eurovision we're talking about. The contest that survived the fall of the Berlin Wall, the dissolution of Yugoslavia, and Jemini's infamous "nul points" wasn't about to let a little global pandemic keep it down. Faster than you could say "Flying the flag," the organizers pivoted, determined to bring some sparkle to a world that suddenly found itself in dire need of a good power ballad.

Enter "Eurovision: Europe Shine a Light," a two-hour spectacle designed to honor the songs and artists of 2020 while bringing Europe together in a time of crisis. It was a bit like attending a Eurovision-themed wake, where we celebrated the contest we'd lost while trying not to cry into our flag-themed cocktails.

Broadcast on May 16, 2020 – the date originally slated for the grand final – this alternative show was hosted by the would-be presenters of Eurovision 2020: Chantal Janzen, Edsilia Rombley, and Jan Smit. All 41 songs that would have competed were featured, albeit in a non-competitive format. It was a participation trophy extravaganza, where everyone was a winner, and the real loser was the virus that shall not be named.

But "Europe Shine a Light" wasn't just about mourning what could have been. It was a celebration of Eurovision's enduring spirit, featuring performances from past winners and fan favorites. From Johnny Logan crooning "What's Another Year" (an eerily appropriate choice) to a continent-wide rendition of Katrina and the Waves' "Love Shine a Light," the show reminded us all why we fell in love with Eurovision in the first place. It felt like a greatest hits album come to life, with a side of pandemic-induced existential crisis.

The response was overwhelming. Over 73 million viewers across 38 markets tuned in, proving that even in the darkest times, the Eurovision flame burns bright.

As the applause faded and the last notes of "Love Shine a Light" echoed across a continent in lockdown, Eurovision fans were left to wonder: what next? The answer, as it turned out, was a rollercoaster ride of hope, uncertainty, and enough hand sanitizer to fill the Rotterdam Ahoy arena.

2021 rolled around, and Eurovision was determined to make its comeback. The slogan "Open Up" took on a whole new meaning as organizers grappled with how to stage an international singing competition in the midst of a global pandemic. It was like trying to run a bubble bath in a tornado – messy, unpredictable, but potentially very entertaining.

The EBU pulled out all the stops to ensure the show could go on. A "Live-On-Tape" contingency plan was put in place, with all acts required to pre-record their performances in case they couldn't make it to Rotterdam. It was Eurovision's version of a safety net, albeit one made of pixels and prayers.

New health and safety measures were implemented faster than you could say "Sanitize your saxophone." The green room became a socially distanced sea of plexiglass and elbow bumps. Delegations were kept in strict "bubbles," leading to jokes about whether some countries might actually perform inside giant hamster balls. (Eurovision organisers: don't get any ideas!)

Despite the challenges, the 2021 contest was a triumph of perseverance, creativity, and the undying human need to watch people sing their hearts out in outrageous costumes. It proved that not even a global pandemic could keep Eurovision down. After all, this is a contest that survived the '80s – COVID-19 didn't stand a chance.

And so, as we emerged blinking into the post-pandemic Eurovision landscape, one thing was clear: the show must – and will – go on. Whether it's through virtual hugs, socially distanced key changes, or performances broadcast from the moon (don't give them ideas), Eurovision will always find a way to unite Europe in music, laughter, and the occasional questionable fashion choice. Now, where did I put my rhinestone-encrusted face mask?

Now, let's talk about the performances that made us forget we were watching Eurovision in the midst of a global crisis. It's as if the contestants looked at the pandemic and said, "Hold my microphone."

Italy's Måneskin strutted onto the 2021 stage with all the swagger of leather-clad rock gods who'd accidentally stumbled into a pop contest. Their win with "Zitti e buoni" was like a shot of espresso in Eurovision's frothy latte – bold, Italian, and leaving everyone slightly jittery. It was as if the ghost of Freddie Mercury had possessed a group of impossibly attractive Italian youngsters and said, "Let's show these pop tarts how it's done."

But if 2021 was the year rock made its comeback, 2022 was the year Eurovision remembered it had a conscience. Ukraine's Kalush Orchestra swept to victory with "Stefania," a song that blended folk motifs with rap faster than you could say "unexpected genre fusion." Their win wasn't just a triumph of musicality; it was a powerful statement of European solidarity in the face of war.

Of course, not every performance could be a winner (this isn't a contest for children, after all), but even the non-victorious entries left their mark. Who could forget Lithuania's The Roop in 2021, whose "Discoteque" dance moves looked like a cross between a TikTok challenge and an interpretive dance about hand sanitizer? Or Norway's Subwoolfer in 2022, proving that even in space, no one can escape the sound of Eurovision?

Now, let's address the elephant in the room – or should I say, the virus in the air? The pandemic didn't just change how we watched Eurovision; it revolutionized how the whole shebang was put together. The contest that once prided itself on cramming as many scantily clad dancers as possible onto a single stage suddenly had to learn the art of social distancing. The production team had to get more creative than a Eurovision lyricist trying to rhyme in English. Staging had to be rethought faster than a quick costume change. Gone were the days of elaborate human pyramids and conga lines. Instead, we got solo artists emoting intensely at cameras, their isolation on stage a poignant reflection of our collective experience. It was deeply moving – or maybe that was just the effect of watching Eurovision sober for once.

But it wasn't all doom and gloom. In 2021 and 2022, to comply with COVID-19 restrictions, the Green Room was expanded to occupy the entire audience standing area - and somehow it looked like participants had even more fun than ever. The pandemic also pushed Eurovision to embrace technology faster than a diva runs towards a wind machine. Augmented reality became the new wind machine, allowing performers to be surrounded by virtual effects that made previous years' pyrotechnics look like a child's sparkler.

The Eurovision app became more essential than ever, allowing fans to engage virtually in ways previously only imaginable. Features like voting, polls, and interactive content made everyone feel like they were right in the heart of the action, all from the comfort of their own home.

In the end, the pandemic might have changed how Eurovision looked, but it couldn't change its heart. The contest proved more resilient than a diva's hairspray, adapting to each new challenge with the grace of a key change and the determination of a power ballad's final chorus.

As we emerged from the pandemic haze, squinting at the bright

lights of a new Eurovision era, one thing was clear: not even
a global crisis could dim the sparkle of this gloriously gaudy,
irrepressibly joyful celebration of music, unity, and the enduring
power of a good key change. Now, where did I put my disco ball
face mask?

The 2020s have seen Eurovision embrace its role as a champion
of diversity and inclusion faster than you can say "douze points to
the non-binary artist." LGBTQ+ representation has been stronger
than ever, both on stage and in the audience. In 2023, Italy's
Marco Mengoni proudly waved the Progress Pride flag during the
Eurovision flag parade, proving that sometimes, a flag can speak
louder than words (or even a key change).

But it's not all rainbows and glitter. The Russia-Ukraine conflict
loomed large over the contest, with Russia excluded from
participation in 2022 and Ukraine unable to host in 2023
despite their win. The organising committee of Eurovision must
suddenly feel like they've found themselves hosting a geopolitical
summit, not a song contest!

The musical landscape of Eurovision in the 2020s has been as
diverse as a Swedish smörgåsbord. We've seen a resurgence of
native language entries, moving away from the dominance of
English faster than you can say "Zitti e buoni." There's been a trend
towards authenticity, with more artists performing self-written
songs that reflect their cultural roots.

But fear not, the classic Eurovision ballad remains a staple,
often blended with modern production techniques. It's like your
grandmother's recipe, but with a sprinkle of EDM and a dash of
TikTok-friendly dance moves.

Speaking of TikTok, the influence of viral music trends has become apparent, with some entries clearly designed to create memorable, shareable moments. It's as if the artists are competing not just for the glass microphone, but for the chance to become the next dancing frog meme.

As for Eurovision's global expansion, Australia's continued participation has opened discussions about further expanding Eurovision beyond Europe's borders. It's as if Eurovision looked at a map and said, "You know what? Let's make this 'Euro' part optional." The launch of the American Song Contest in 2022 and plans for Eurovision Canada demonstrate the brand's global ambitions. Soon, we might need to rename it "Worldvision" (trademark pending).

International viewership continues to grow, particularly through online streaming. Eurovision parties and screening events have become popular worldwide, from Brazil to Japan, showcasing the contest's universal appeal. It's as if the whole world has collectively decided that what they really need in their lives is more glitter, wind machines, and inexplicable prop choices.

Behind the scenes, the pandemic necessitated significant adaptations in organization and production. Enhanced health and safety protocols became standard practice faster than you could say "socially distanced key change." The role of technology in coordinating a multinational event of this scale has become even more crucial. It's as if Eurovision decided to embrace the digital age and said, "You know what? Let's make this more complicated than explaining the voting system to your grandma."

The European Broadcasting Union (EBU) has had to navigate

increasingly complex geopolitical situations while maintaining the contest's apolitical stance. This has led to ongoing debates about the boundaries between cultural expression and political statements within Eurovision. It's a balancing act more precarious than a performer in 8-inch heels on a rotating platform.

As we sashay towards the future, one thing is clear: Eurovision continues to evolve, balancing its rich traditions with the need to stay relevant in a rapidly changing world. It's like a glittery chameleon, adapting to its surroundings while never losing its essential sparkle. So grab your scorecards, practice your most dramatic gasp, and get ready for whatever fabulous madness Eurovision has in store for us next. After all, in Eurovision, the show must always go on – preferably with more pyrotechnics, more outlandish costumes, and at least one performance that leaves you wondering, "Did that really just happen?" The future is calling, and Eurovision is ready to answer – just as soon as it finishes applying one last layer of glitter.

Fashion and staging in this era became more inventive than a drag queen's makeup bag. With pandemic restrictions limiting the number of people on stage, artists had to get creative faster than you can say "costume change." We saw more augmented reality than a Pokemon Go convention, with virtual effects that made previous years' pyrotechnics look like a damp sparkler. It was as if Eurovision had decided to embrace the digital age and said, "You know what? Let's make this more complicated than explaining the voting system to your grandma."

Speaking of complications, let's talk controversies, shall we? Because it wouldn't be Eurovision without a dash of drama to go with our key changes. The Belarusian entry disqualification in 2021 upped the drama levels to new heights; I think Belarus had looked at the rulebook and said, "Guidelines? More like suggestions, darling." But the EBU was not amused and showed them the door faster than you can say "nul points." Their entry was perceived as having a political message that went against the contest's apolitical nature and was deemed a violation by the EBU. Despite the opportunity to submit a revised version or a new song, Belarus failed to comply with the EBU's requests.

But the show must go on, and go on it did! The future of Eurovision looks brighter than a sequined jumpsuit under a spotlight. The contest has proven more adaptable than a pop star's political views, embracing new technologies and formats with the enthusiasm of a fan discovering the Eurovision drinking game for the first time.

Potential format changes are being whispered about in the corridors of the EBU louder than the gossip at the after-party. Could we see more integration of social media? Perhaps a TikTok dance challenge round? Or maybe a "Eurovision: Unplugged" where artists have to perform without their trusty backing tracks.

As we sashay towards the future, one thing is clear: Eurovision continues to evolve, balancing its rich traditions with the need to stay relevant in a rapidly changing world. It's like a glittery chameleon, adapting to its surroundings while never losing its essential sparkle.

The contest's enduring appeal lies in its ability to unite Europe (and Australia, because why not?) in a celebration of music, diversity, and the enduring power of a good key change. It's a reminder that even in the darkest times, we can come together, raise our voices (and our glowsticks), and create something beautiful.

So, as we close this chapter and look to the future, let's raise a glass of whatever fabulous cocktail you're sipping. Here's to Eurovision - may it continue to dazzle, delight, and occasionally bewilder us for many years to come. After all, in a world of uncertainty, we can always count on Eurovision to bring us together in a riot of music, sequins, and inexplicable prop choices. Now, where did I put my disco ball face mask? The next Eurovision party is just around the corner, and darling, I intend to be ready!

Eurovision Winners Of The 2020S

Year	Host City	Winner (Country)	Song Title
2020	*Cancelled*	*N/A*	*N/A*
2021	Rotterdam	Måneskin (Italy)	Zitti e buoni
2022	Turin	Kalush Orchestra (Ukraine)	Stefania
2023	Liverpool	Loreen (Sweden)	Tattoo
2024	Malmö	Nemo (Switzerland)	The Code
2025	Basel	*TBC*	*TBC*

Did You Know?

- The 2020 contest was the first in Eurovision history to be cancelled, due to the COVID-19 pandemic. A special program, "Eurovision: Europe Shine a Light," was broadcast instead, honoring the songs and artists that would have competed.
- Måneskin's 2021 win was investigated after the final due to rumours of drug use in the green room. Damiano David, the band's front man, later took a drug test, which came up negative.
- Although Ukraine won the 2022 contest, they were unable to host the 2023 event due to the ongoing war. The United Kingdom, who were the runners-up in 2022, hosted instead.

CHAPTER 9: BEHIND THE CURTAIN

O kay, buckle up! We're about to take a fabulous journey behind the sequined curtain of Eurovision. It's time to peek into the glittery underbelly of this beast we call the Song Contest. Prepare yourselves for a rollercoaster ride through the chaos, drama, and sheer fabulousness that happens when you try to corral dozens of divas, hundreds of crew members, and enough hairspray to single-handedly deplete the ozone layer.

First things first, let's talk about the Eurovision hunger games, otherwise known as the host city bidding process. It's like a competition to see who can empty their coffers incredibly quickly. The criteria for selecting a host city are more complex than explaining the voting system to your grandma. Does the city have a suitable venue? Can it accommodate thousands of flag-waving fans? Is there enough glitter in the country's national reserves? These are the burning questions that keep EBU executives up at night.

Once a city wins this dubious honor, the real fun begins.

Transforming an arena into a Eurovision wonderland is like trying to turn a pumpkin into something extraordinary, only with more pyrotechnics and less magic. The venue needs to be big enough to house not just the performers, but also their egos. And let's not forget the green room, which needs to comfortably fit 26 acts, their entourages, and enough nervous energy to power a small country.

The host broadcaster suddenly finds themselves in the hot seat, juggling more balls than a circus performer. They're responsible for everything from camera angles to catering, all while trying to showcase their country in the best possible light. It's like throwing the world's biggest house party, but with better music and more spandex.

Meanwhile, the EBU watches over the proceedings like a benevolent but slightly terrifying fairy godmother. They're there to ensure everything runs smoothly, or at least as smoothly as possible when you're dealing with a show that once featured a man in a hamster wheel. The EBU's rulebook is thicker than a Eurovision diva's makeup, covering everything from song length to the acceptable size of a wind machine.

Behind the scenes, an army of unsung heroes works tirelessly to bring the Eurovision magic to life. There are more job titles than there are keys in a Swedish pop song. From the stage managers coordinating every movement to the sound engineers making sure we can hear every last key change, these are the people who truly make Eurovision happen. They're the ones running around with headsets, clipboards, and enough coffee in their systems to fuel a rocket launch.

And let's not forget the evolution of Eurovision aesthetics. We've come a long way from the days when a sparkly dress and a wind machine were considered the height of sophistication. Now, we have LED screens the size of small countries, enough pyrotechnics to worry the fire department, and costumes that look like they were designed by a committee of drag queens on acid. It's fabulous, darling, absolutely fabulous.

The rehearsal schedule leading up to the big night is more grueling than a boot camp run by a glitter-obsessed drill sergeant. Performers run through their acts more times than there are key changes in a Moldovan folk-pop fusion number. It's during these rehearsals that the real drama unfolds. Will the pyrotechnics go off at the right moment? Can the dancer pull off that death-defying backflip in 6-inch heels? Will someone remember to plug in the wind machine? These are the questions that keep Eurovision fans on the edge of their seats.

As we pause for a brief intermission in our behind-the-scenes tour, remember: what you see on stage is just the tip of the sequined iceberg. There's a whole world of chaos, creativity, and hairspray abuse happening behind that curtain. So the next time you watch Eurovision, spare a thought for the army of fabulous individuals working tirelessly to bring this glittery spectacle to your screen. Now, where did I put my bedazzled headset? These pyrotechnics aren't going to coordinate themselves!

Now: the Green Room. This hallowed space has evolved from a simple waiting area to a pressure cooker of emotions, where you can cut the tension with a sequined knife. It's where dreams are made, crushed, and occasionally drowned in complimentary champagne. Over the years, we've seen everything from nervous breakdowns to impromptu conga lines. It's like a reality show within a reality show, only with better lighting and more flag-waving. This space can have a huge psychological impact on the performers.

Speaking of waving, let's talk about the security measures that would make Fort Knox look like a garden shed. With thousands of fans from across Europe (and Australia, because why not?) descending on the host city, security teams have their work cut out for them. It's a delicate balance between maintaining safety and not dampening the party spirit. It shows just how important the event is. After all, nothing says "Eurovision" quite like a glitter-covered metal detector.

And let's not forget the logistical nightmare of coordinating delegations from dozens of countries. It's like herding cats, if the cats were wearing 6-inch heels and had very specific dietary requirements. From transportation to accommodation, every detail must be perfect. Heaven forbid a diva doesn't get their requested brand of mineral water – it could cause an international incident!

Now, brace yourselves for some number crunching, because hosting Eurovision costs more than a lifetime supply of wind machines. The budget for a modern Eurovision could probably fund a small country's space program. But fear not! Sponsors line up incredibly quickly, eager to slap their logo on anything that doesn't move (and some things that do).

Behind every great Eurovision performance is an equally great (or at least equally stressed) press team. The press center is a hive of activity, buzzing with more energy than a Swedish pop banger. Journalists from around the world descend like glitter-seeking missiles, ready to dissect every performance, every costume choice, and every awkward presenter joke. In the age of social media, the press team's job has become more demanding than a diva with a 12-page rider. One wrong tweet and suddenly you're trending for all the wrong reasons.

But it's not all stress and hairspray backstage. The Eurovision family is real, darlings, and the bonds formed in the trenches of this glittery war are unbreakable. We've heard tales of unlikely friendships, last-minute collaborations, and parties that would make Gatsby blush. There was the time when a power outage led to an impromptu acoustic jam session, or when a missing prop led to a frantic continent-wide search. These are the moments that don't make it to our screens but make Eurovision the beautiful, chaotic mess we all know and love.

As the glitter settles and the last key change fades away, the host city is left to sweep up the remnants of Eurovision madness. But the impact lasts long after the delegations have packed up their sequins and gone home. Host cities often see a boost in tourism, as fans flock to walk in the footsteps of their Eurovision idols. Local businesses ride the Eurovision wave, selling everything from themed cocktails to knockoff trophy-shaped souvenirs.

In the end, what happens behind the curtain is just as magical, if not more so, than what we see on stage. It's a testament to the power of music, the spirit of cooperation (most of the time), and the unifying force of a good key change. Eurovision is more than just a song contest – it's a glitter-covered, key-change-filled, wind-machine-powered miracle that somehow comes together year after year.

So the next time you watch Eurovision, spare a thought for the army of unsung heroes working tirelessly behind the scenes. They're the ones who turn chaos into choreography, panic into pyrotechnics, and a simple stage into a wonderland of light and sound. They are the true Eurovision stars, darling – even if they're not the ones taking a bow at the end of the night.

Now, if you'll excuse me, I need to go practice my wind machine technique. These feathers won't blow themselves, you know!

CHAPTER 10: THE POLITICS OF EUROVISION

Buckle up your sequined seatbelts and prepare for a rollercoaster ride through the glittery minefield of Eurovision politics! You thought this was just a singing competition? It's a diplomatic summit with better costumes and more key changes. From neighborly love to long-standing feuds, Eurovision has always been a fascinating reflection of Europe's complex political landscape, often serving as a microcosm of geopolitical tensions and a unique platform for cultural expression – and protest.

Let's start with the elephant in the room - or should I say, the bear in the arena? Russia's exclusion from the 2022 contest following its invasion of Ukraine set a precedent. Even in the land of wind machines and power ballads, some lines you just don't cross. This demonstrated that Eurovision, despite its light-hearted nature, exists within a broader political context and it often reflects geopolitical fault lines.

But Russia's exclusion is just one chapter in Eurovision's long and complicated relationship with politics. Back in 2009, Georgia got its knuckles rapped for its subtle-as-a-sledgehammer entry "We Don't Wanna Put In." The EBU deemed it too political. Perhaps Georgia should have tried something a bit more subtle rather than something akin to showing up to a black-tie event wearing a t-shirt with Putin's face crossed out. If you're going to throw shade, at least bedazzle it first!

Speaking of not-so-subtle shade, let's talk voting blocs. The Nordic countries stick together like sequins on a jumpsuit. Greece and Cyprus? They're the original Eurovision BFFs, exchanging "douze points" like friendship bracelets. It's not just about the music; it's a complex tapestry of shared history, cultural connections, and perhaps the occasional backroom deal involving a lifetime supply of feta cheese.

But it's not all "douze points" diplomacy and Scandi-love. Some countries bring more baggage to Eurovision than a diva with a 12-piece orchestra. Armenia and Azerbaijan? Their Eurovision drama could fuel a Netflix series for years. This isn't just friendly rivalry; it's a reflection of a deep-seated conflict that spills onto the Eurovision stage with the force of a glitter cannon.

The tension between these two nations has simmered on the Eurovision stage ever since they both debuted in the contest. In 2008, Azerbaijan included images of Nagorno-Karabakh, a disputed territory at the heart of their conflict, in their stage show. Armenia protested, and the EBU, playing the role of Eurovision referee, stepped in and asked Azerbaijan to remove the images. It seems even in Eurovision, some political statements go too far and need to be reigned in.

The following year, Armenia retaliated, subtly (or not so subtly) displaying images of "We Are Our Mountains", a monument in Nagorno-Karabakh, during their performance. Azerbaijan responded by blurring the monument during the Armenian spokesperson's voting announcement. It was a Eurovision tit-for-tat, played out on live television, demonstrating that no matter how much Eurovision pretends to be apolitical, some conflicts just can't be contained by sequins and wind machines.

The 2009 contest also saw accusations of voting irregularities. Azerbaijan launched an investigation into its own citizens who voted for the Armenian entry. Imagine the interrogation: "So, you like their song, huh? Really? Explain yourself." Armenia, in turn, claimed that Azerbaijan had censored their performance by switching the broadcast to local programming during their song. The EBU must have felt like the headteacher breaking up a playground fight, only with more glitter and fewer tears.

The Armenia-Azerbaijan conflict isn't just a sideshow; it's a reminder of Eurovision's unique position as a cultural battleground. Where else can you see geopolitical tensions played out through power ballads and wind machines? It's a bizarre and occasionally unsettling mix of politics, pop, and enough drama to rival a soap opera.

Moving on from regional feuds, let's talk about the language debate. Once upon a time, Eurovision was a linguistic smorgasbord, where Italian arias battled it out against Finnish folk songs. Then, in 1999, the EBU unleashed the English-language kraken, and Eurovision transformed into a pop music melting pot. Some celebrated, others mourned, but one thing's for sure: the language debate has been a constant key change in

Eurovision's history.

But don't think for a second that singing in English is a guaranteed ticket to Eurovision glory. Just ask Ukraine's Go_A, whose 2021 entry "Shum," sung partially in Ukrainian, proved that you can still make a splash (and a political statement) even if most of Europe doesn't understand a word you're singing.

Hosting Eurovision is a political act in itself, requiring not just a killer stage but also some serious diplomatic maneuvering. When Ukraine triumphed in 2022 but couldn't host due to the war, the UK stepped up to the plate. It was a heartwarming moment of solidarity, proving that sometimes, Eurovision can put aside politics and embrace the power of shared humanity (and a good key change).

Eurovision has become a champion of social causes, waving the flag for LGBTQ+ rights with all the subtlety of a rainbow-colored wind machine. Conchita Wurst's victory in 2014 was a watershed moment. It was like Eurovision collectively looked at its reputation as a queer icon and decided, "Let's crank up the fabulous!"

Speaking of cranking things up, the politics of host city selection deserve its own ballad. Whilst the previous winning country (almost always) hosts, the bidding by cities within those countries can be more competitive than a "nul points" survival contest. Cities spend millions, promising everything from state-of-the-art arenas to complimentary glitter for every attendee. For instance, the 2017 Eurovision Song Contest saw a fierce bidding war between several Ukrainian cities, with Kiev ultimately emerging victorious due to its promise of a revamped International

Exhibition Centre and a city-wide Eurovision makeover.

Looking ahead, keeping Eurovision apolitical seems about as likely as a UK victory post-Brexit. It's a contest that reflects the world, warts and all. But in its own sparkly, chaotic way, Eurovision also reminds us that music can transcend borders, unite communities, and perhaps even achieve world peace (or at least a temporary ceasefire in the green room).

Now, if you'll excuse me, I need to go practice my diplomatic dance moves. These voting blocs aren't going to form themselves, you know.

CHAPTER 11: EUROVISION'S TECHNOLOGICAL EVOLUTION

L et's dive back into Eurovision's technological evolution, darlings. From its beginnings as a rather static television broadcast to the complex digital spectacle of the modern era, the contest has consistently pushed the boundaries of what's possible in broadcasting – and often with more than a little bit of help from some very questionable fashion choices.

In the early days of 1956, Eurovision was a television broadcast that was more akin to a slightly stuffy radio show with pictures. It's hard for us to imagine this now, but in that era, it was a significant achievement in broadcasting and international cooperation. Imagine trying to convey the fabulousness of a Eurovision performance through a grainy, slightly wobbly black and white camera. But, despite these significant limitations, the contest persevered, and soon, it made a huge step up - by the addition of colour.

The arrival of colour television introduced a whole new world of possibilities, meaning that performers suddenly had to consider not just their performance, but how they looked on screen. The early days of black-and-white TV were like watching Eurovision through a vintage Instagram filter. But the introduction of colour was like suddenly turning the lights on, meaning that performers could finally showcase their true colours - literally! The 1974 performance of "Waterloo" was a perfect example of this shift.

Then came the great orchestra debate. Once upon a time, every Eurovision performance was backed by a live orchestra. It was all very classy and sophisticated, like a musical version of a fancy dinner party. But, as the '90s rolled around, pre-recorded backing tracks started to sneak in like uninvited guests. By 1999, the live orchestra had been replaced by backing tracks, much to the chagrin of purists, but to the delight of producers, who now had a better chance of keeping things in tune.

As sound technology improved, Eurovision moved on from microphones that were bigger than most of today's phones to sleek and almost invisible devices that would make James Bond jealous. The sound mixing became increasingly sophisticated, and meant that even the most pitch-challenged performers could be made to sound like angels. As for the visuals - they went from simple backdrops and a bit of dry ice to LED screens the size of small countries, lighting rigs that could rival a space launch, and enough pyrotechnics to worry the fire department of a small city.

Stage design also became a crucial element of the performance, moving on from simple risers to elaborate constructions, often featuring complex and moving parts. It was as though someone had decided that the only way to truly appreciate a power ballad was to make it into a Bond-level spectacle of choreography and flashing lights.

The evolution of voting methods in the Eurovision Song Contest mirrors the technological advancements of the times, transitioning from handwritten scores to national televoting and, eventually, to app-based systems. This digital transformation hasn't always been seamless. In 2019, the Belarusian jury was caught attempting to manipulate the digital ballot box, revealing their preferred rankings before the final and casting doubt on the integrity of the voting process. This scandal led to their votes being discarded and replaced with an aggregate score, underscoring the vulnerabilities of the modern voting process. In an era of big data, maintaining secrecy is a challenge, and this incident highlighted both the limitations and the significance of technology in the contest's voting infrastructure.

The digital revolution also changed the way that fans could follow and engage with the contest. It was as if the internet was created for Eurovision fans, as social media allows us to dissect every performance, discuss every costume choice, and share our opinions with a global community, all in real time. Platforms like Twitter, Instagram, and TikTok became essential, making the show feel interactive and more accessible than ever before.

And it's still evolving! Eurovision has now started to dip its sequined toes into the world of virtual and augmented reality, and other futuristic technologies. It seems that the contest will continue to develop and adopt all that modern technology has to offer, and the only limit to this is our imagination. The pandemic also forced the contest to innovate, and the introduction of virtual performances and "Live-on-Tape" systems gave us a glimpse of an alternate version of Eurovision that was equal parts impressive and slightly bizarre.

The core of Eurovision will always be the music, the spectacle, and the unifying power of a good key change. But, thanks to a constant evolution of technology, the contest is now a glittering and utterly unique celebration of music, performance, and the sheer power of broadcasting. And the next step in this development is the impact that it has had on music itself.

CHAPTER 12: EUROVISION'S EFFECT ON POPULAR MUSIC

From ABBA to Måneskin, Eurovision has launched careers, sparked trends, and left its indelible mark on the world of popular music. But how exactly has this glittery contest, often dismissed as kitsch, managed to influence the global music landscape? Let's dive into the complex, often surprising, and always entertaining relationship between Eurovision and pop music.

For decades, the contest has served as a launchpad for aspiring artists, a showcase for diverse musical styles, and a barometer of ever-evolving pop trends. But its influence extends far beyond the three minutes of each performance. Eurovision has shaped careers, sparked trends, and left an indelible mark on the music industry, even if the impact isn't always immediately obvious.

The Launchpad Effect: From Eurovision Stage To Global Stardom

Let's start with the most obvious effect: Eurovision's ability to launch artists into the international spotlight. The list of Eurovision alumni who have gone on to achieve success is a testament to the contest's power as a talent incubator.

Of course, the name that instantly springs to mind is ABBA. The Swedish quartet's 1974 victory with "Waterloo" wasn't just a contest win, it was a pop-culture explosion. ABBA's success transcended national borders and linguistic barriers, transforming them into a worldwide phenomenon, and setting the template for future Eurovision success stories. Their catchy melodies, innovative production, and unforgettable performances continue to resonate with audiences worldwide, and their enduring popularity is a testament to the power of a truly great Eurovision song.

But ABBA isn't the only example of a Eurovision act to achieve superstardom. Celine Dion, who represented Switzerland in 1988 with "Ne partez pas sans moi," went on to become one of the best-selling music artists of all time. Her soaring vocals and power ballad prowess, first showcased on the Eurovision stage, became her trademark, leading to a career that has spanned decades. She was evidence that Eurovision could, in fact, launch careers.

And let's not forget Cliff Richard, who represented the UK in both 1968 and 1973, who, while not actually winning the contest, certainly used the exposure to boost his already impressive career. Similarly, Nana Mouskouri, who represented Luxembourg in 1963, used the Eurovision stage as a springboard to a very successful career on the international stage. They are just a couple of examples of artists who used the reach of the contest to achieve longevity in the music business.

More recently, Måneskin, the Italian rock band who took the 2021 crown with "Zitti e buoni," injected a much-needed dose of rock and roll into the contest. Their victory catapulted them onto the world stage, resulting in sold-out tours and charting hits. They proved that Eurovision could be a platform for more than just pop, and they managed to transcend the contest and make a huge impact on modern rock music.

These artists demonstrate that Eurovision can be more than a quirky contest. It can be a legitimate launchpad for international careers, providing exposure to millions of viewers and the chance to showcase their talent on a large scale. While not every Eurovision winner will become a sensation, the contest can certainly act as a springboard for those with enough talent, determination, and perhaps a dash of Eurovision magic.

The Elusive "Eurovision Sound"

So, what exactly is the "Eurovision sound," and how has it influenced popular music? This is a question that has baffled critics and delighted fans for decades. It's a constantly evolving mix of musical styles, trends, and traditions that is hard to define, but instantly recognizable.

In the early days, Eurovision was dominated by traditional ballads, often performed with a full orchestra. This sound, while sometimes seen as a bit dated by today's standards, played a key role in shaping the contest's identity and establishing a musical heritage. As time went on, Eurovision embraced a much wider range of sounds. The disco era saw an explosion of catchy, danceable tunes. The 80s brought us synth-pop and power ballads, each with their own distinctive energy. The 90s saw a collision of pop, rock, and ethnic influences and, of course, the four-on-the-floor dance anthems of the new millennium. And then we entered the age of genre-bending, and we started to see everything from hard-rock to folk-rap to jazz-infused pop.

Despite all of these changes, the "Eurovision Sound" can be identified by a few key characteristics. Catchy melodies, dramatic key changes, and sing-along choruses seem to be essential. Many songs incorporate multiple languages, even when English is the primary language for the performance. And let's not forget the importance of a soaring, emotional vocal performance, often complete with a final chorus that reaches for the heavens.

Of course, this doesn't always align with mainstream music trends. Some critics have dismissed the "Eurovision sound" as cheesy or formulaic, which is a fairly popular opinion outside of the fan-base! However, it has definitely influenced pop music both in Europe and further afield. Many Eurovision songs have gone on to become international hits, proving that the contest has a knack for identifying (or creating) music that resonates with a broad audience. Songs like "Volare," "Making Your Mind Up," "Save Your Kisses for Me," and "Hallelujah" all achieved international success, and all were (at one point or another) Eurovision songs.

Beyond The Winners: The Influence Of Non-Winning Entries

It's worth noting that Eurovision's effect on popular music isn't limited to the winners. Many non-winning entries have also made a significant impact, often becoming fan favorites and cult classics. Domenico Modugno's "Volare" is a perfect example of a non-winning entry that went on to become more successful than the actual winner in 1958. This early example of a contest hit which failed to win the competition highlighted one of the big questions about Eurovision, what actually constitutes a "winning song?"

The contest also has a habit of highlighting emerging trends, offering a platform for new artists and styles that may not be recognised elsewhere. Many Eurovision entries become viral sensations long after the contest, with various performances being circulated online and used as memes. This goes to show the contest's influence in the social media age and its ability to entertain far beyond the three minutes on stage.

The influence of non-winners also extends to the careers of many artists. While many will fade into obscurity after the contest, for many others it can be a valuable career boost. Even if they don't win, a Eurovision performance can give artists a broad platform, and it's this exposure that can be used to achieve lasting success.

The National Impact: Eurovision And The Rise Of Homegrown Talent

Beyond the worldwide impact, Eurovision also plays a significant role in the development of national music industries. For many countries, it provides a rare opportunity to showcase their unique musical traditions to an international audience. The contest can also create opportunities for collaborations between artists and producers, while generating valuable revenue for their country through tourism, merchandise, and increased music sales.

For some smaller nations, Eurovision is their only opportunity to access the music scene. Artists from countries with less established music industries can use Eurovision as a platform to make a name for themselves internationally. This is especially true in the digital age, when Eurovision performances are easily accessible to a broad audience. The reach of social media and streaming means that a song that might not have been heard outside of a small country a few decades ago, can now go viral overnight.

❖ ❖ ❖

Ultimately, Eurovision's effect on popular music is far from straightforward. It's a complex and constantly evolving relationship that is hard to quantify, but definitely worth exploring. The contest has produced superstars, shaped musical trends, and provided a platform for national music industries, and in doing so has cemented itself in popular music history. It might not always be taken seriously by the mainstream music industry, but its influence is undeniable. As Eurovision continues to evolve, it is only certain that its impact on the world of popular music will remain an interesting, and incredibly important, part of its ongoing story.

CHAPTER 13: EUROVISION AND EUROPEAN IDENTITY

For over six decades, Eurovision has been more than just a song contest; it's a mirror reflecting the ever-changing face of Europe. From post-war hopes for unity to the complexities of modern identity, the contest has both shaped and been shaped by the social, political, and cultural landscape of the continent. But does Eurovision truly represent a shared European identity, or is it something far more fragmented, more contested, more... interesting?

A Stage For Unity? The Promise And The Reality

In the aftermath of World War II, the founders of Eurovision envisioned a contest that could bring Europe together, promoting cultural exchange and fostering a sense of shared identity. The idea was that by harmonising (literally and figuratively) across national borders, Europeans could find common ground and move beyond past conflicts. It was a noble goal, and in many ways, Eurovision has lived up to that ideal.

The contest provides a unique platform for countries to showcase their cultures, languages, and traditions to an international audience. Through the power of music, Eurovision has helped to break down cultural barriers, allowing Europeans to experience the rich diversity of their continent. It has also created shared memories and experiences, as millions of viewers gather each year to watch the spectacle unfold. Who can forget the four-way tie of 1969, or the skirt-ripping theatrics of Bucks Fizz, or the monster-masked madness of Lordi? These are moments that have become part of a collective European cultural consciousness.

However, the reality of Eurovision and its impact on European identity is far more nuanced than a simple story of unity. While the contest may bring Europeans together to celebrate music and culture, it also highlights existing divisions and tensions. The concept of "Europe" itself is a complex and contested one, and Eurovision serves as a mirror, reflecting both the hopes and the anxieties surrounding the European project.

A Celebration Of Diversity? Or A Stage For Stereotypes?

Eurovision is often lauded for its celebration of diversity, showcasing the wide range of musical styles, languages, and cultures found across the continent. From traditional folk music to contemporary pop, from soaring ballads to electrifying rock anthems, the contest has always been a showcase for Europe's rich and varied cultural tapestry.

However, the way in which this diversity is represented has not always been without its critics. Some have accused Eurovision of promoting stereotypes, reducing national cultures to a collection of cliches. The over-reliance on certain musical genres, the use of traditional costumes, and the occasional "folklore" performance has led some to question whether Eurovision really celebrates diversity, or simply perpetuates caricatures.

The language debate also raises questions about cultural identity. While Eurovision has allowed participants to sing in various languages, English has increasingly become the dominant force in the contest. Some argue that this linguistic homogenization undermines the diversity of European cultures, while others see it as a pragmatic response to the demands of a globalized world. It's like a complex web of languages all getting a pop makeover, but with a lingering sense that maybe not all languages are created equal in the world of Eurovision.

The Politics Of Identity: Voting Blocs And National Pride

And let's not forget the political dimension of Eurovision and European identity. The voting patterns of the contest, often influenced by geographical proximity and cultural ties, can highlight existing alliances and divisions among European countries. The phenomenon of "neighbourly voting" has become a well-established part of the contest's folklore, with countries reliably exchanging "douze points" to their nearby friends. While this can be seen as a celebration of regional solidarity, it also raises questions about whether the contest is truly about musical merit, or simply a reflection of political relationships. It has become a way for countries to express their existing political ties through the voting process.

For many countries, Eurovision is more than just a song contest; it is a platform for national branding and a source of national pride. It is an opportunity to showcase their culture, their music, and their unique identity to an international audience. The contest can also spark intense national debates, raising questions about the nature of national identity and the way in which it is represented on the world stage.

This sense of national pride can sometimes clash with the ideals of European unity, creating tensions between local and continental identities. Some nations, eager to showcase their own uniqueness, may be reluctant to embrace a shared "European" identity. This is especially true for nations that have experienced complicated historical relationships with other European countries.

Language, Representation, And The Quest For A Shared Identity

The question of language has always been central to the debates surrounding Eurovision and European identity. The switch from national language requirements to the free language rule has led to a significant shift in the linguistic landscape of the contest. English, with its global reach and relatively easy access, has become the lingua franca of Eurovision.

While this has led to more commercially successful songs, it has also raised concerns about the marginalization of national languages and cultural traditions. Some countries have actively resisted this trend, choosing to perform in their native tongues, while others have embraced a more multilingual approach, blending English with their own national languages.

The issues of representation and diversity are also central to the debate surrounding Eurovision and European identity. The contest has made progress in terms of LGBTQ+ representation, showcasing a wider range of gender identities and sexual orientations. However, there is still work to be done in terms of ethnic diversity, both on stage and in the audience.

◆ ◆ ◆

As we pause for a brief intermission in our exploration of Eurovision and European identity, remember this: the contest is not a simple story of unity and diversity. It is a complex and often contradictory phenomenon that reflects the hopes, anxieties, and tensions surrounding the idea of "Europe." It is a stage where individual nations showcase their unique cultures, but also one where Europeans come together to celebrate their shared love of music, spectacle, and the enduring power of a good key change. The complexities and contradictions of Eurovision reflect the complexities and contradictions of Europe itself.

CHAPTER 14: THE FUTURE OF EUROVISION

The future of Eurovision? It's as unpredictable as a live performance, as dazzling as a sequined jumpsuit, and as full of potential as a power ballad's final chorus. From the rise of streaming to the expansion of the contest beyond Europe's borders, let's explore the challenges, opportunities, and fabulous possibilities that lie ahead for our beloved contest.

Challenges And Opportunities In The Streaming Era

The rise of digital streaming has revolutionized the music industry, and Eurovision is no exception. In the past, a Eurovision win could guarantee radio play, chart success, and a place in pop culture history. But in the streaming era, success is measured in clicks, views, and shares. This presents both challenges and opportunities for the contest.

On one hand, streaming provides a platform for Eurovision artists to reach a wider global audience than ever before. Songs can go viral overnight, reaching millions of listeners outside of the traditional Eurovision fanbase. This can lead to unexpected success stories, giving artists a chance to build international careers even if they don't win the contest.

On the other hand, the streaming era has also increased competition. The internet is saturated with music, and it can be difficult for even the most catchy Eurovision song to stand out from the crowd. For the songs to continue to achieve recognition the producers are forced to be more innovative with staging, marketing, and promotion to secure a place on the global playlist.

Potential Format Changes And Expansions

As we look to the future, it's likely that we will see more format changes to the contest. The introduction of the semi-finals was a significant change, and it's not impossible that the contest could adopt a multi-stage format. Perhaps we might see the introduction of "wild card" entries, selected by an online vote, or maybe even a separate competition for non-European countries. Who knows? In the world of Eurovision, anything is possible!

The EBU is constantly experimenting with new technologies and formats to engage a new audience. Interactive elements, virtual reality experiences, and enhanced social media integration could become an essential part of the Eurovision experience. The contest will need to continue to find new ways to create a global viewing experience, while maintaining the core aspects that make it so loved. The key for the future is to balance the traditions of the contest with the need to remain relevant in a rapidly changing world.

The Global Reach Of Eurovision

And speaking of a global audience, it's time to address the growing international appeal of the Eurovision Song Contest. What began as a European cultural experiment has now blossomed into a global phenomenon, attracting millions of viewers from all corners of the world.

Australia's participation in the contest has proven that Eurovision's appeal transcends geographical boundaries. The country's love for the contest and the passion of the fans have cemented their place in the Eurovision family. Their success in the competition shows the appeal of Eurovision to an audience that exists way beyond the European continent.

The popularity of Eurovision parties and screening events around the world is a testament to the contest's global appeal. From Brazil to Japan, fans gather to celebrate music, culture, and the unique energy that only Eurovision can bring. The contest's accessibility through streaming services and social media has further expanded its reach, allowing fans from all corners of the world to participate in the Eurovision experience.

The launch of the "American Song Contest" and "Eurovision

Canada" shows the ambition to expand the brand outside of Europe. This represents both a huge opportunity and also a potential risk to the original contest. It will be interesting to see if this will expand the Eurovision brand into a globally recognised franchise, or dilute its unique and much loved characteristics.

As Eurovision looks to the future, it will need to adapt to the demands of a truly global audience. This will likely involve some format changes, as well as considering the diverse needs and interests of an international audience. It will be interesting to see what this will mean for the future of the original contest.

Eurovision's Role In A Changing World

Looking beyond the music, it's also worth considering Eurovision's role in a changing Europe and a changing world. The contest has always been a reflection of the political and cultural climate, and in recent years, this has become more apparent than ever. The contest has had to address the conflict in Ukraine and the rise in social consciousness about diversity and representation. These events have highlighted the way that Eurovision has now grown into a reflection of, and an influence on, global politics and social issues.

As we move forward, it's likely that Eurovision will continue to be a platform for discussion on important social and political issues. The contest will need to strike a delicate balance, ensuring it remains a celebration of music and culture while also engaging with pressing global issues. This might mean supporting certain social movements, or banning certain entries that are seen as politically motivated, but, whatever the future holds, Eurovision will need to keep evolving to remain relevant in a fast-moving world.

As we gaze into the future, one thing is certain: Eurovision will continue to surprise us, delight us, and occasionally bewilder us with its unique blend of music, spectacle, and cultural commentary. The contest has always been a chameleon, adapting to changing times and embracing new challenges with the same energy it brings to a dramatic key change.

So, as we prepare for the next chapter in Eurovision's grand story, let's do it with open minds, open hearts, and a willingness to embrace the unexpected. The future is calling, and it's time to answer with all the glitter, wind machines, and off-key charm we can muster! Now, where did I put my crystal ball (and my bedazzled headset)? The future isn't going to predict itself!

CHAPTER 15: THE ENDURING APPEAL OF EUROVISION

Why do we watch it? Why do we love it? Why do we spend weeks arguing about key changes and wind machines? Eurovision's enduring appeal is a complex and multifaceted phenomenon, one that goes far beyond the glitter and the glam. From the power of music to the sense of community, let's explore the magic that keeps us coming back for more, year after year.

A Celebration Of Music And Spectacle

At its heart, Eurovision is a celebration of music. It's a chance to discover new artists, explore diverse musical styles, and belt out your favorite songs along with millions of other fans across the globe. The contest is a testament to the power of music to transcend borders, languages, and cultural differences.

But Eurovision is more than just a song contest; it's a spectacle. It's a dazzling display of creativity, featuring elaborate costumes, dramatic staging, and enough pyrotechnics to make a rock concert blush. It's a place where the mundane is replaced with the magnificent, and where the ordinary transforms into the extraordinary. It's a chance to escape from the everyday and immerse yourself in a world of glitter, wind machines, and the occasional key change. It's a sensory overload that keeps us coming back for more year after year.

A Unique Cultural Phenomenon

Beyond the music and the spectacle, Eurovision is a unique cultural phenomenon. It's a reflection of the ever-changing political and social landscape of Europe and the world. It's a stage where national identities are put on display, and where conversations about cultural diversity, representation, and inclusivity unfold. It's a living, breathing history lesson, told through the medium of pop music.

The contest has also become a cultural touchstone, creating shared memories and experiences for generations of viewers. Whether you're a die-hard fan who has watched every contest since 1956, or a casual observer who tunes in for the spectacle, Eurovision has a unique way of weaving its way into our lives. It's a topic of conversation, a source of joy, and an event that sparks passionate debates around the world.

The Emotional Connection: Community And

Belonging

Perhaps one of the most significant reasons for Eurovision's enduring appeal is the emotional connection that fans have with the contest. It's a space where people from all backgrounds and walks of life come together to share their love for music, performance, and the occasional moment of glorious absurdity.

For many, Eurovision is more than just a show; it's a community. It's a place to connect with like-minded individuals, express your true self, and feel a sense of belonging. The shared experience of watching the contest, whether in person or from the comfort of your own living room, creates a sense of connection that transcends geographical boundaries. It's a place where fans can embrace their inner diva, wave their flags with pride, and sing their hearts out, no matter how off-key they might be.

A Constantly Evolving Spectacle

Eurovision's enduring appeal also lies in its ability to constantly evolve. The contest has never been afraid to embrace new technologies, explore new musical styles, and address pressing social issues. It's a chameleon, always adapting to changing times and remaining relevant in a fast-paced world.

From the early days of black-and-white television to the digital streaming era, Eurovision has always pushed boundaries and defied expectations. It's a contest that has managed to stay true to its roots while also embracing the future. It's a reminder that sometimes the greatest traditions are the ones that are willing to change.

The Global Fanbase And The Power Of "Eurovision Magic"

And let's not forget the global fan base that has helped propel Eurovision to the status of a worldwide phenomenon. From Sydney to Sao Paulo, Eurovision parties and screening events unite people from all over the globe in a shared love for this unique cultural event. The passion of the fans, their creativity, and their unwavering support are what truly make Eurovision shine.

Ultimately, the enduring appeal of Eurovision lies in its ability to make us feel something. It's a contest that can make us laugh, cry, cheer, and occasionally cringe, all within the space of three minutes. It's a reminder that even in a world of division and conflict, we can always come together to celebrate music, culture, and the sheer joy of performance.

◆ ◆ ◆

As we bring our Eurovision journey to a close, let's raise a glass to the contest that has, for over six decades, brought us music, magic, and a healthy dose of glorious absurdity. The show will continue to evolve, to adapt, and to keep on surprising us, but one thing remains certain: the enduring appeal of Eurovision will keep on shining, bringing people together for many years to come.

Now, where did I put my scorecards, my flag, and my most dramatic sequined outfit? Because it's always time for Eurovision!

CLOSE - THE HEART OF EUROVISION

For all its glitter and glam, for all its soaring vocals and dramatic staging, the heart of Eurovision, for me, has always been about connection. It's about the shared experience, the passionate debates, and the collective joy that comes from experiencing something so unique, so utterly Eurovision. It's a reminder that even in a world that often feels divided, music still has the power to bring us together. It's a community, a family, a feeling - and one that I will always cherish.

Writing this book has been a journey in itself, a deep dive into a world I've adored for so long. It's been a joy to revisit the iconic performances, the memorable moments, and the quirky controversies that have made Eurovision what it is today. More than just a recounting of events, it has been a chance to explore the contest's remarkable ability to reflect the times, influence popular culture, and create a sense of belonging for millions around the world. I hope that in these pages, we've managed to capture some of the magic that makes Eurovision so special, and that you feel as connected to this world as I do.

The show must, and always will, go on. May the music continue to unite us.